Name_____

A.
```
  4     3     2     5     3     0     4     1     2     5
x 3   x 1   x 2   x 5   x 5   x 3   x 2   x 4   x 0   x 2
```

B.
```
  5     4     0     4     1     2     5     2     0     3
x 5   x 2   x 5   x 4   x 5   x 3   x 4   x 5   x 1   x 3
```

C.
```
  0     3     5     4     3     1     2     0     4     1
x 2   x 1   x 1   x 5   x 0   x 1   x 2   x 1   x 0   x 2
```

D.
```
  2     3     2     5     2     4     0     3     5     1
x 3   x 4   x 0   x 3   x 5   x 4   x 0   x 1   x 2   x 2
```

E.
```
  5     1     2     3     0     4     3     1     3     5
x 0   x 3   x 1   x 2   x 2   x 1   x 4   x 0   x 5   x 1
```

F.
```
  2     0     0     4     3     1     1     4     3     0
x 4   x 5   x 0   x 2   x 3   x 5   x 1   x 1   x 0   x 4
```

G.
```
  5     2     0     1     5     4     1     2     5     2
x 4   x 1   x 0   x 5   x 0   x 4   x 2   x 5   x 1   x 4
```

H.
```
  4     5     1     3     3     1     5     0     2     4
x 0   x 2   x 4   x 0   x 2   x 3   x 3   x 1   x 2   x 3
```

I.
```
  4     0     3     4     1     2     3     2     1     5
x 5   x 3   x 2   x 3   x 1   x 3   x 5   x 1   x 4   x 5
```

J.
```
  3     1     5     4     5     0     4     1     2     3
x 4   x 0   x 4   x 1   x 3   x 4   x 5   x 3   x 4   x 3
```

Y0-CAR-214

Minutes | 1 | 2 | 3 | 4 | 5 | **Score** [ ]

1

Multiplication Facts: 0 to 5

A.
$$\begin{array}{c}1\\ \times\,3\end{array}\quad \begin{array}{c}2\\ \times\,5\end{array}\quad \begin{array}{c}1\\ \times\,4\end{array}\quad \begin{array}{c}4\\ \times\,3\end{array}\quad \begin{array}{c}4\\ \times\,5\end{array}\quad \begin{array}{c}0\\ \times\,1\end{array}\quad \begin{array}{c}3\\ \times\,3\end{array}\quad \begin{array}{c}4\\ \times\,0\end{array}\quad \begin{array}{c}2\\ \times\,3\end{array}\quad \begin{array}{c}3\\ \times\,4\end{array}$$

B.
$$\begin{array}{c}0\\ \times\,5\end{array}\quad \begin{array}{c}5\\ \times\,5\end{array}\quad \begin{array}{c}4\\ \times\,1\end{array}\quad \begin{array}{c}2\\ \times\,4\end{array}\quad \begin{array}{c}1\\ \times\,1\end{array}\quad \begin{array}{c}5\\ \times\,2\end{array}\quad \begin{array}{c}4\\ \times\,4\end{array}\quad \begin{array}{c}2\\ \times\,1\end{array}\quad \begin{array}{c}3\\ \times\,0\end{array}\quad \begin{array}{c}5\\ \times\,3\end{array}$$

C.
$$\begin{array}{c}5\\ \times\,1\end{array}\quad \begin{array}{c}0\\ \times\,3\end{array}\quad \begin{array}{c}3\\ \times\,4\end{array}\quad \begin{array}{c}2\\ \times\,3\end{array}\quad \begin{array}{c}1\\ \times\,5\end{array}\quad \begin{array}{c}4\\ \times\,0\end{array}\quad \begin{array}{c}3\\ \times\,2\end{array}\quad \begin{array}{c}5\\ \times\,2\end{array}\quad \begin{array}{c}1\\ \times\,3\end{array}\quad \begin{array}{c}1\\ \times\,2\end{array}$$

D.
$$\begin{array}{c}2\\ \times\,0\end{array}\quad \begin{array}{c}3\\ \times\,3\end{array}\quad \begin{array}{c}5\\ \times\,1\end{array}\quad \begin{array}{c}0\\ \times\,5\end{array}\quad \begin{array}{c}3\\ \times\,1\end{array}\quad \begin{array}{c}4\\ \times\,5\end{array}\quad \begin{array}{c}4\\ \times\,2\end{array}\quad \begin{array}{c}0\\ \times\,0\end{array}\quad \begin{array}{c}1\\ \times\,1\end{array}\quad \begin{array}{c}5\\ \times\,5\end{array}$$

E.
$$\begin{array}{c}4\\ \times\,4\end{array}\quad \begin{array}{c}2\\ \times\,2\end{array}\quad \begin{array}{c}1\\ \times\,0\end{array}\quad \begin{array}{c}4\\ \times\,1\end{array}\quad \begin{array}{c}4\\ \times\,3\end{array}\quad \begin{array}{c}0\\ \times\,2\end{array}\quad \begin{array}{c}3\\ \times\,5\end{array}\quad \begin{array}{c}2\\ \times\,1\end{array}\quad \begin{array}{c}5\\ \times\,0\end{array}\quad \begin{array}{c}5\\ \times\,3\end{array}$$

F.
$$\begin{array}{c}1\\ \times\,5\end{array}\quad \begin{array}{c}3\\ \times\,3\end{array}\quad \begin{array}{c}0\\ \times\,1\end{array}\quad \begin{array}{c}2\\ \times\,5\end{array}\quad \begin{array}{c}1\\ \times\,4\end{array}\quad \begin{array}{c}2\\ \times\,2\end{array}\quad \begin{array}{c}4\\ \times\,5\end{array}\quad \begin{array}{c}0\\ \times\,4\end{array}\quad \begin{array}{c}3\\ \times\,0\end{array}\quad \begin{array}{c}3\\ \times\,5\end{array}$$

G.
$$\begin{array}{c}2\\ \times\,4\end{array}\quad \begin{array}{c}1\\ \times\,2\end{array}\quad \begin{array}{c}4\\ \times\,1\end{array}\quad \begin{array}{c}1\\ \times\,1\end{array}\quad \begin{array}{c}5\\ \times\,2\end{array}\quad \begin{array}{c}2\\ \times\,3\end{array}\quad \begin{array}{c}3\\ \times\,1\end{array}\quad \begin{array}{c}4\\ \times\,3\end{array}\quad \begin{array}{c}3\\ \times\,2\end{array}\quad \begin{array}{c}0\\ \times\,3\end{array}$$

H.
$$\begin{array}{c}2\\ \times\,1\end{array}\quad \begin{array}{c}3\\ \times\,0\end{array}\quad \begin{array}{c}5\\ \times\,1\end{array}\quad \begin{array}{c}1\\ \times\,3\end{array}\quad \begin{array}{c}3\\ \times\,5\end{array}\quad \begin{array}{c}4\\ \times\,0\end{array}\quad \begin{array}{c}5\\ \times\,4\end{array}\quad \begin{array}{c}0\\ \times\,2\end{array}\quad \begin{array}{c}5\\ \times\,5\end{array}\quad \begin{array}{c}0\\ \times\,1\end{array}$$

I.
$$\begin{array}{c}0\\ \times\,4\end{array}\quad \begin{array}{c}4\\ \times\,2\end{array}\quad \begin{array}{c}5\\ \times\,3\end{array}\quad \begin{array}{c}2\\ \times\,2\end{array}\quad \begin{array}{c}2\\ \times\,4\end{array}\quad \begin{array}{c}1\\ \times\,0\end{array}\quad \begin{array}{c}3\\ \times\,4\end{array}\quad \begin{array}{c}5\\ \times\,4\end{array}\quad \begin{array}{c}2\\ \times\,0\end{array}\quad \begin{array}{c}1\\ \times\,4\end{array}$$

J.
$$\begin{array}{c}4\\ \times\,2\end{array}\quad \begin{array}{c}0\\ \times\,0\end{array}\quad \begin{array}{c}5\\ \times\,0\end{array}\quad \begin{array}{c}3\\ \times\,2\end{array}\quad \begin{array}{c}1\\ \times\,5\end{array}\quad \begin{array}{c}3\\ \times\,1\end{array}\quad \begin{array}{c}5\\ \times\,4\end{array}\quad \begin{array}{c}2\\ \times\,5\end{array}\quad \begin{array}{c}1\\ \times\,2\end{array}\quad \begin{array}{c}4\\ \times\,4\end{array}$$

Minutes

1	2	3	4	5

Score

A.
6	0	7	5	3	7	1	4	4	5
x 2	x 5	x 5	x 6	x 3	x 3	x 5	x 4	x 6	x 4

B.
3	7	2	1	3	2	6	4	0	7
x 0	x 7	x 3	x 1	x 6	x 5	x 5	x 1	x 2	x 5

C.
6	3	4	7	1	4	5	2	7	3
x 5	x 6	x 3	x 1	x 0	x 7	x 3	x 2	x 6	x 5

D.
5	1	5	3	4	0	6	4	2	6
x 7	x 4	x 0	x 2	x 3	x 0	x 1	x 5	x 7	x 2

E.
2	5	7	0	4	6	4	3	2	7
x 1	x 3	x 4	x 4	x 2	x 6	x 5	x 2	x 5	x 0

F.
7	3	2	5	1	3	5	0	3	6
x 2	x 5	x 4	x 5	x 6	x 4	x 2	x 7	x 7	x 4

G.
5	4	0	6	6	2	2	7	1	2
x 4	x 2	x 1	x 7	x 3	x 6	x 7	x 7	x 3	x 2

H.
1	7	6	4	5	2	5	4	3	6
x 2	x 3	x 6	x 4	x 2	x 0	x 7	x 6	x 1	x 7

I.
6	3	1	7	6	5	0	6	2	3
x 0	x 4	x 7	x 4	x 3	x 1	x 3	x 4	x 4	x 3

J.
4	2	7	2	0	4	5	3	5	7
x 0	x 3	x 6	x 6	x 6	x 7	x 5	x 7	x 6	x 2

Minutes					**Score**
1	2	3	4	5	

Name_____

A.
   6   1   7   4   0   4   5   3   3   5
  x 6   x 3   x 0   x 2   x 5   x 4   x 6   x 2   x 6   x 4

B.
   6   5   1   3   7   3   4   0   6   2
  x 5   x 1   x 7   x 7   x 4   x 2   x 6   x 2   x 1   x 6

C.
   4   3   7   2   5   1   7   6   4   7
  x 5   x 3   x 7   x 4   x 6   x 0   x 2   x 3   x 7   x 6

D.
   5   0   3   6   3   6   7   1   4   5
  x 5   x 0   x 1   x 7   x 5   x 4   x 5   x 2   x 0   x 7

E.
   7   2   6   4   3   0   4   5   7   4
  x 3   x 0   x 2   x 5   x 1   x 4   x 7   x 2   x 1   x 3

F.
   1   5   6   3   4   5   4   3   0   4
  x 5   x 3   x 0   x 7   x 3   x 7   x 1   x 4   x 7   x 2

G.
   7   2   6   0   5   2   3   6   4   1
  x 7   x 5   x 4   x 1   x 4   x 1   x 4   x 7   x 1   x 6

H.
   4   6   2   5   1   7   5   3   3   7
  x 4   x 2   x 3   x 0   x 1   x 6   x 2   x 0   x 6   x 3

I.
   2   3   6   1   6   7   0   7   2   6
  x 1   x 3   x 1   x 4   x 6   x 1   x 3   x 4   x 7   x 5

J.
   7   0   5   5   7   2   6   4   5   3
  x 5   x 6   x 1   x 3   x 2   x 2   x 3   x 6   x 5   x 5

Minutes

1	2	3	4	5

Score

A.
$$\begin{array}{r}8\\ \times\,0\\ \hline\end{array}\quad \begin{array}{r}5\\ \times\,2\\ \hline\end{array}\quad \begin{array}{r}0\\ \times\,4\\ \hline\end{array}\quad \begin{array}{r}9\\ \times\,2\\ \hline\end{array}\quad \begin{array}{r}4\\ \times\,5\\ \hline\end{array}\quad \begin{array}{r}2\\ \times\,7\\ \hline\end{array}\quad \begin{array}{r}7\\ \times\,6\\ \hline\end{array}\quad \begin{array}{r}3\\ \times\,6\\ \hline\end{array}\quad \begin{array}{r}6\\ \times\,7\\ \hline\end{array}\quad \begin{array}{r}1\\ \times\,1\\ \hline\end{array}$$

B.
$$\begin{array}{r}5\\ \times\,8\\ \hline\end{array}\quad \begin{array}{r}2\\ \times\,3\\ \hline\end{array}\quad \begin{array}{r}6\\ \times\,4\\ \hline\end{array}\quad \begin{array}{r}4\\ \times\,2\\ \hline\end{array}\quad \begin{array}{r}9\\ \times\,7\\ \hline\end{array}\quad \begin{array}{r}0\\ \times\,9\\ \hline\end{array}\quad \begin{array}{r}3\\ \times\,1\\ \hline\end{array}\quad \begin{array}{r}7\\ \times\,3\\ \hline\end{array}\quad \begin{array}{r}1\\ \times\,6\\ \hline\end{array}\quad \begin{array}{r}8\\ \times\,4\\ \hline\end{array}$$

C.
$$\begin{array}{r}7\\ \times\,5\\ \hline\end{array}\quad \begin{array}{r}9\\ \times\,1\\ \hline\end{array}\quad \begin{array}{r}1\\ \times\,4\\ \hline\end{array}\quad \begin{array}{r}6\\ \times\,1\\ \hline\end{array}\quad \begin{array}{r}2\\ \times\,0\\ \hline\end{array}\quad \begin{array}{r}5\\ \times\,3\\ \hline\end{array}\quad \begin{array}{r}9\\ \times\,9\\ \hline\end{array}\quad \begin{array}{r}4\\ \times\,3\\ \hline\end{array}\quad \begin{array}{r}9\\ \times\,5\\ \hline\end{array}\quad \begin{array}{r}0\\ \times\,3\\ \hline\end{array}$$

D.
$$\begin{array}{r}2\\ \times\,8\\ \hline\end{array}\quad \begin{array}{r}6\\ \times\,6\\ \hline\end{array}\quad \begin{array}{r}4\\ \times\,7\\ \hline\end{array}\quad \begin{array}{r}0\\ \times\,1\\ \hline\end{array}\quad \begin{array}{r}7\\ \times\,9\\ \hline\end{array}\quad \begin{array}{r}3\\ \times\,3\\ \hline\end{array}\quad \begin{array}{r}5\\ \times\,5\\ \hline\end{array}\quad \begin{array}{r}1\\ \times\,2\\ \hline\end{array}\quad \begin{array}{r}4\\ \times\,0\\ \hline\end{array}\quad \begin{array}{r}8\\ \times\,1\\ \hline\end{array}$$

E.
$$\begin{array}{r}0\\ \times\,6\\ \hline\end{array}\quad \begin{array}{r}8\\ \times\,8\\ \hline\end{array}\quad \begin{array}{r}3\\ \times\,5\\ \hline\end{array}\quad \begin{array}{r}8\\ \times\,3\\ \hline\end{array}\quad \begin{array}{r}2\\ \times\,2\\ \hline\end{array}\quad \begin{array}{r}5\\ \times\,1\\ \hline\end{array}\quad \begin{array}{r}1\\ \times\,7\\ \hline\end{array}\quad \begin{array}{r}4\\ \times\,8\\ \hline\end{array}\quad \begin{array}{r}7\\ \times\,0\\ \hline\end{array}\quad \begin{array}{r}3\\ \times\,9\\ \hline\end{array}$$

F.
$$\begin{array}{r}7\\ \times\,1\\ \hline\end{array}\quad \begin{array}{r}2\\ \times\,6\\ \hline\end{array}\quad \begin{array}{r}8\\ \times\,5\\ \hline\end{array}\quad \begin{array}{r}1\\ \times\,3\\ \hline\end{array}\quad \begin{array}{r}6\\ \times\,0\\ \hline\end{array}\quad \begin{array}{r}3\\ \times\,2\\ \hline\end{array}\quad \begin{array}{r}5\\ \times\,7\\ \hline\end{array}\quad \begin{array}{r}0\\ \times\,8\\ \hline\end{array}\quad \begin{array}{r}6\\ \times\,3\\ \hline\end{array}\quad \begin{array}{r}2\\ \times\,4\\ \hline\end{array}$$

G.
$$\begin{array}{r}2\\ \times\,9\\ \hline\end{array}\quad \begin{array}{r}9\\ \times\,0\\ \hline\end{array}\quad \begin{array}{r}0\\ \times\,2\\ \hline\end{array}\quad \begin{array}{r}5\\ \times\,4\\ \hline\end{array}\quad \begin{array}{r}4\\ \times\,4\\ \hline\end{array}\quad \begin{array}{r}7\\ \times\,8\\ \hline\end{array}\quad \begin{array}{r}1\\ \times\,0\\ \hline\end{array}\quad \begin{array}{r}6\\ \times\,9\\ \hline\end{array}\quad \begin{array}{r}3\\ \times\,0\\ \hline\end{array}\quad \begin{array}{r}9\\ \times\,4\\ \hline\end{array}$$

H.
$$\begin{array}{r}8\\ \times\,9\\ \hline\end{array}\quad \begin{array}{r}2\\ \times\,1\\ \hline\end{array}\quad \begin{array}{r}5\\ \times\,9\\ \hline\end{array}\quad \begin{array}{r}7\\ \times\,4\\ \hline\end{array}\quad \begin{array}{r}0\\ \times\,5\\ \hline\end{array}\quad \begin{array}{r}4\\ \times\,1\\ \hline\end{array}\quad \begin{array}{r}3\\ \times\,7\\ \hline\end{array}\quad \begin{array}{r}9\\ \times\,8\\ \hline\end{array}\quad \begin{array}{r}1\\ \times\,9\\ \hline\end{array}\quad \begin{array}{r}8\\ \times\,7\\ \hline\end{array}$$

I.
$$\begin{array}{r}4\\ \times\,6\\ \hline\end{array}\quad \begin{array}{r}9\\ \times\,6\\ \hline\end{array}\quad \begin{array}{r}1\\ \times\,8\\ \hline\end{array}\quad \begin{array}{r}6\\ \times\,5\\ \hline\end{array}\quad \begin{array}{r}3\\ \times\,4\\ \hline\end{array}\quad \begin{array}{r}5\\ \times\,0\\ \hline\end{array}\quad \begin{array}{r}2\\ \times\,5\\ \hline\end{array}\quad \begin{array}{r}8\\ \times\,2\\ \hline\end{array}\quad \begin{array}{r}0\\ \times\,0\\ \hline\end{array}\quad \begin{array}{r}7\\ \times\,7\\ \hline\end{array}$$

J.
$$\begin{array}{r}1\\ \times\,5\\ \hline\end{array}\quad \begin{array}{r}9\\ \times\,3\\ \hline\end{array}\quad \begin{array}{r}6\\ \times\,2\\ \hline\end{array}\quad \begin{array}{r}0\\ \times\,7\\ \hline\end{array}\quad \begin{array}{r}8\\ \times\,6\\ \hline\end{array}\quad \begin{array}{r}5\\ \times\,6\\ \hline\end{array}\quad \begin{array}{r}4\\ \times\,9\\ \hline\end{array}\quad \begin{array}{r}3\\ \times\,8\\ \hline\end{array}\quad \begin{array}{r}7\\ \times\,2\\ \hline\end{array}\quad \begin{array}{r}6\\ \times\,8\\ \hline\end{array}$$

Minutes

1	2	3	4	5

Score

A.
$\begin{array}{r} 8 \\ \times 2 \\ \hline \end{array}$
$\begin{array}{r} 4 \\ \times 8 \\ \hline \end{array}$
$\begin{array}{r} 1 \\ \times 3 \\ \hline \end{array}$
$\begin{array}{r} 6 \\ \times 7 \\ \hline \end{array}$
$\begin{array}{r} 3 \\ \times 0 \\ \hline \end{array}$
$\begin{array}{r} 9 \\ \times 3 \\ \hline \end{array}$
$\begin{array}{r} 2 \\ \times 4 \\ \hline \end{array}$
$\begin{array}{r} 5 \\ \times 6 \\ \hline \end{array}$
$\begin{array}{r} 0 \\ \times 4 \\ \hline \end{array}$
$\begin{array}{r} 7 \\ \times 5 \\ \hline \end{array}$

B.
$\begin{array}{r} 7 \\ \times 2 \\ \hline \end{array}$
$\begin{array}{r} 2 \\ \times 9 \\ \hline \end{array}$
$\begin{array}{r} 6 \\ \times 0 \\ \hline \end{array}$
$\begin{array}{r} 9 \\ \times 6 \\ \hline \end{array}$
$\begin{array}{r} 0 \\ \times 2 \\ \hline \end{array}$
$\begin{array}{r} 3 \\ \times 7 \\ \hline \end{array}$
$\begin{array}{r} 5 \\ \times 9 \\ \hline \end{array}$
$\begin{array}{r} 4 \\ \times 6 \\ \hline \end{array}$
$\begin{array}{r} 8 \\ \times 5 \\ \hline \end{array}$
$\begin{array}{r} 1 \\ \times 5 \\ \hline \end{array}$

C.
$\begin{array}{r} 4 \\ \times 1 \\ \hline \end{array}$
$\begin{array}{r} 8 \\ \times 8 \\ \hline \end{array}$
$\begin{array}{r} 0 \\ \times 7 \\ \hline \end{array}$
$\begin{array}{r} 6 \\ \times 4 \\ \hline \end{array}$
$\begin{array}{r} 5 \\ \times 2 \\ \hline \end{array}$
$\begin{array}{r} 9 \\ \times 4 \\ \hline \end{array}$
$\begin{array}{r} 1 \\ \times 0 \\ \hline \end{array}$
$\begin{array}{r} 7 \\ \times 8 \\ \hline \end{array}$
$\begin{array}{r} 2 \\ \times 8 \\ \hline \end{array}$
$\begin{array}{r} 3 \\ \times 3 \\ \hline \end{array}$

D.
$\begin{array}{r} 5 \\ \times 3 \\ \hline \end{array}$
$\begin{array}{r} 6 \\ \times 8 \\ \hline \end{array}$
$\begin{array}{r} 2 \\ \times 3 \\ \hline \end{array}$
$\begin{array}{r} 8 \\ \times 4 \\ \hline \end{array}$
$\begin{array}{r} 4 \\ \times 3 \\ \hline \end{array}$
$\begin{array}{r} 1 \\ \times 8 \\ \hline \end{array}$
$\begin{array}{r} 7 \\ \times 4 \\ \hline \end{array}$
$\begin{array}{r} 0 \\ \times 0 \\ \hline \end{array}$
$\begin{array}{r} 3 \\ \times 6 \\ \hline \end{array}$
$\begin{array}{r} 9 \\ \times 1 \\ \hline \end{array}$

E.
$\begin{array}{r} 3 \\ \times 4 \\ \hline \end{array}$
$\begin{array}{r} 1 \\ \times 6 \\ \hline \end{array}$
$\begin{array}{r} 9 \\ \times 0 \\ \hline \end{array}$
$\begin{array}{r} 5 \\ \times 7 \\ \hline \end{array}$
$\begin{array}{r} 0 \\ \times 5 \\ \hline \end{array}$
$\begin{array}{r} 8 \\ \times 9 \\ \hline \end{array}$
$\begin{array}{r} 6 \\ \times 6 \\ \hline \end{array}$
$\begin{array}{r} 7 \\ \times 1 \\ \hline \end{array}$
$\begin{array}{r} 2 \\ \times 0 \\ \hline \end{array}$
$\begin{array}{r} 4 \\ \times 5 \\ \hline \end{array}$

F.
$\begin{array}{r} 0 \\ \times 9 \\ \hline \end{array}$
$\begin{array}{r} 9 \\ \times 8 \\ \hline \end{array}$
$\begin{array}{r} 3 \\ \times 1 \\ \hline \end{array}$
$\begin{array}{r} 7 \\ \times 7 \\ \hline \end{array}$
$\begin{array}{r} 2 \\ \times 5 \\ \hline \end{array}$
$\begin{array}{r} 6 \\ \times 1 \\ \hline \end{array}$
$\begin{array}{r} 4 \\ \times 0 \\ \hline \end{array}$
$\begin{array}{r} 1 \\ \times 2 \\ \hline \end{array}$
$\begin{array}{r} 8 \\ \times 7 \\ \hline \end{array}$
$\begin{array}{r} 5 \\ \times 5 \\ \hline \end{array}$

G.
$\begin{array}{r} 6 \\ \times 5 \\ \hline \end{array}$
$\begin{array}{r} 3 \\ \times 9 \\ \hline \end{array}$
$\begin{array}{r} 0 \\ \times 1 \\ \hline \end{array}$
$\begin{array}{r} 9 \\ \times 7 \\ \hline \end{array}$
$\begin{array}{r} 4 \\ \times 2 \\ \hline \end{array}$
$\begin{array}{r} 5 \\ \times 1 \\ \hline \end{array}$
$\begin{array}{r} 1 \\ \times 1 \\ \hline \end{array}$
$\begin{array}{r} 8 \\ \times 1 \\ \hline \end{array}$
$\begin{array}{r} 2 \\ \times 2 \\ \hline \end{array}$
$\begin{array}{r} 7 \\ \times 9 \\ \hline \end{array}$

H.
$\begin{array}{r} 5 \\ \times 8 \\ \hline \end{array}$
$\begin{array}{r} 1 \\ \times 4 \\ \hline \end{array}$
$\begin{array}{r} 7 \\ \times 3 \\ \hline \end{array}$
$\begin{array}{r} 3 \\ \times 5 \\ \hline \end{array}$
$\begin{array}{r} 9 \\ \times 5 \\ \hline \end{array}$
$\begin{array}{r} 2 \\ \times 7 \\ \hline \end{array}$
$\begin{array}{r} 4 \\ \times 9 \\ \hline \end{array}$
$\begin{array}{r} 6 \\ \times 2 \\ \hline \end{array}$
$\begin{array}{r} 8 \\ \times 3 \\ \hline \end{array}$
$\begin{array}{r} 0 \\ \times 8 \\ \hline \end{array}$

I.
$\begin{array}{r} 2 \\ \times 1 \\ \hline \end{array}$
$\begin{array}{r} 8 \\ \times 6 \\ \hline \end{array}$
$\begin{array}{r} 7 \\ \times 0 \\ \hline \end{array}$
$\begin{array}{r} 1 \\ \times 9 \\ \hline \end{array}$
$\begin{array}{r} 9 \\ \times 9 \\ \hline \end{array}$
$\begin{array}{r} 4 \\ \times 4 \\ \hline \end{array}$
$\begin{array}{r} 0 \\ \times 3 \\ \hline \end{array}$
$\begin{array}{r} 7 \\ \times 6 \\ \hline \end{array}$
$\begin{array}{r} 3 \\ \times 2 \\ \hline \end{array}$
$\begin{array}{r} 5 \\ \times 4 \\ \hline \end{array}$

J.
$\begin{array}{r} 4 \\ \times 7 \\ \hline \end{array}$
$\begin{array}{r} 0 \\ \times 6 \\ \hline \end{array}$
$\begin{array}{r} 6 \\ \times 9 \\ \hline \end{array}$
$\begin{array}{r} 3 \\ \times 8 \\ \hline \end{array}$
$\begin{array}{r} 5 \\ \times 0 \\ \hline \end{array}$
$\begin{array}{r} 2 \\ \times 6 \\ \hline \end{array}$
$\begin{array}{r} 8 \\ \times 0 \\ \hline \end{array}$
$\begin{array}{r} 9 \\ \times 2 \\ \hline \end{array}$
$\begin{array}{r} 1 \\ \times 7 \\ \hline \end{array}$
$\begin{array}{r} 6 \\ \times 3 \\ \hline \end{array}$

Minutes

1	2	3	4	5

Score

Name_____ **Multiplication Facts: 0 to 9**

A.
$$9 \times 7 \quad 4 \times 8 \quad 3 \times 9 \quad 6 \times 5 \quad 1 \times 0 \quad 6 \times 2 \quad 2 \times 3 \quad 8 \times 2 \quad 1 \times 6 \quad 7 \times 0$$

B.
$$2 \times 6 \quad 5 \times 5 \quad 0 \times 3 \quad 8 \times 7 \quad 3 \times 3 \quad 4 \times 0 \quad 9 \times 9 \quad 0 \times 8 \quad 6 \times 9 \quad 7 \times 6$$

C.
$$7 \times 9 \quad 4 \times 3 \quad 7 \times 3 \quad 2 \times 0 \quad 7 \times 5 \quad 0 \times 0 \quad 1 \times 3 \quad 9 \times 5 \quad 4 \times 5 \quad 2 \times 7$$

D.
$$1 \times 7 \quad 9 \times 3 \quad 3 \times 2 \quad 0 \times 9 \quad 5 \times 8 \quad 8 \times 0 \quad 2 \times 2 \quad 4 \times 9 \quad 5 \times 0 \quad 8 \times 6$$

E.
$$4 \times 7 \quad 3 \times 8 \quad 2 \times 9 \quad 6 \times 1 \quad 5 \times 2 \quad 1 \times 2 \quad 6 \times 8 \quad 9 \times 1 \quad 0 \times 4 \quad 6 \times 3$$

F.
$$3 \times 5 \quad 5 \times 4 \quad 0 \times 6 \quad 7 \times 8 \quad 4 \times 2 \quad 2 \times 8 \quad 7 \times 1 \quad 3 \times 4 \quad 0 \times 7 \quad 8 \times 1$$

G.
$$8 \times 5 \quad 3 \times 1 \quad 8 \times 3 \quad 0 \times 1 \quad 5 \times 7 \quad 9 \times 8 \quad 1 \times 5 \quad 4 \times 4 \quad 9 \times 4 \quad 2 \times 5$$

H.
$$0 \times 5 \quad 9 \times 6 \quad 6 \times 0 \quad 3 \times 7 \quad 2 \times 1 \quad 8 \times 8 \quad 6 \times 4 \quad 1 \times 8 \quad 9 \times 0 \quad 6 \times 6$$

I.
$$7 \times 7 \quad 5 \times 9 \quad 3 \times 0 \quad 7 \times 2 \quad 1 \times 1 \quad 4 \times 1 \quad 6 \times 7 \quad 5 \times 3 \quad 8 \times 9 \quad 1 \times 9$$

J.
$$2 \times 4 \quad 5 \times 6 \quad 1 \times 4 \quad 4 \times 6 \quad 8 \times 4 \quad 3 \times 6 \quad 5 \times 1 \quad 0 \times 2 \quad 7 \times 4 \quad 9 \times 2$$

Minutes

1	2	3	4	5

Score

A.
$$\begin{array}{cc} 8 \\ \times 3 \end{array}$$
$$\begin{array}{cc} 9 \\ \times 6 \end{array}$$
$$\begin{array}{cc} 4 \\ \times 6 \end{array}$$
$$\begin{array}{cc} 9 \\ \times 0 \end{array}$$
$$\begin{array}{cc} 1 \\ \times 2 \end{array}$$
$$\begin{array}{cc} 3 \\ \times 3 \end{array}$$
$$\begin{array}{cc} 0 \\ \times 8 \end{array}$$
$$\begin{array}{cc} 9 \\ \times 3 \end{array}$$
$$\begin{array}{cc} 5 \\ \times 4 \end{array}$$
$$\begin{array}{cc} 2 \\ \times 4 \end{array}$$

B.
$$\begin{array}{cc} 1 \\ \times 6 \end{array}$$
$$\begin{array}{cc} 7 \\ \times 6 \end{array}$$
$$\begin{array}{cc} 0 \\ \times 6 \end{array}$$
$$\begin{array}{cc} 5 \\ \times 1 \end{array}$$
$$\begin{array}{cc} 4 \\ \times 2 \end{array}$$
$$\begin{array}{cc} 3 \\ \times 8 \end{array}$$
$$\begin{array}{cc} 7 \\ \times 3 \end{array}$$
$$\begin{array}{cc} 0 \\ \times 2 \end{array}$$
$$\begin{array}{cc} 6 \\ \times 4 \end{array}$$
$$\begin{array}{cc} 5 \\ \times 9 \end{array}$$

C.
$$\begin{array}{cc} 8 \\ \times 6 \end{array}$$
$$\begin{array}{cc} 2 \\ \times 8 \end{array}$$
$$\begin{array}{cc} 8 \\ \times 0 \end{array}$$
$$\begin{array}{cc} 1 \\ \times 3 \end{array}$$
$$\begin{array}{cc} 6 \\ \times 2 \end{array}$$
$$\begin{array}{cc} 5 \\ \times 7 \end{array}$$
$$\begin{array}{cc} 2 \\ \times 1 \end{array}$$
$$\begin{array}{cc} 6 \\ \times 8 \end{array}$$
$$\begin{array}{cc} 3 \\ \times 5 \end{array}$$
$$\begin{array}{cc} 8 \\ \times 9 \end{array}$$

D.
$$\begin{array}{cc} 7 \\ \times 9 \end{array}$$
$$\begin{array}{cc} 1 \\ \times 1 \end{array}$$
$$\begin{array}{cc} 0 \\ \times 4 \end{array}$$
$$\begin{array}{cc} 7 \\ \times 2 \end{array}$$
$$\begin{array}{cc} 4 \\ \times 5 \end{array}$$
$$\begin{array}{cc} 3 \\ \times 2 \end{array}$$
$$\begin{array}{cc} 5 \\ \times 0 \end{array}$$
$$\begin{array}{cc} 9 \\ \times 5 \end{array}$$
$$\begin{array}{cc} 0 \\ \times 9 \end{array}$$
$$\begin{array}{cc} 8 \\ \times 2 \end{array}$$

E.
$$\begin{array}{cc} 4 \\ \times 3 \end{array}$$
$$\begin{array}{cc} 1 \\ \times 7 \end{array}$$
$$\begin{array}{cc} 9 \\ \times 8 \end{array}$$
$$\begin{array}{cc} 6 \\ \times 7 \end{array}$$
$$\begin{array}{cc} 0 \\ \times 1 \end{array}$$
$$\begin{array}{cc} 2 \\ \times 7 \end{array}$$
$$\begin{array}{cc} 7 \\ \times 5 \end{array}$$
$$\begin{array}{cc} 3 \\ \times 7 \end{array}$$
$$\begin{array}{cc} 2 \\ \times 3 \end{array}$$
$$\begin{array}{cc} 4 \\ \times 1 \end{array}$$

F.
$$\begin{array}{cc} 3 \\ \times 4 \end{array}$$
$$\begin{array}{cc} 2 \\ \times 5 \end{array}$$
$$\begin{array}{cc} 1 \\ \times 8 \end{array}$$
$$\begin{array}{cc} 8 \\ \times 5 \end{array}$$
$$\begin{array}{cc} 6 \\ \times 3 \end{array}$$
$$\begin{array}{cc} 5 \\ \times 6 \end{array}$$
$$\begin{array}{cc} 9 \\ \times 4 \end{array}$$
$$\begin{array}{cc} 2 \\ \times 0 \end{array}$$
$$\begin{array}{cc} 9 \\ \times 9 \end{array}$$
$$\begin{array}{cc} 1 \\ \times 5 \end{array}$$

G.
$$\begin{array}{cc} 8 \\ \times 8 \end{array}$$
$$\begin{array}{cc} 0 \\ \times 7 \end{array}$$
$$\begin{array}{cc} 9 \\ \times 1 \end{array}$$
$$\begin{array}{cc} 3 \\ \times 9 \end{array}$$
$$\begin{array}{cc} 6 \\ \times 1 \end{array}$$
$$\begin{array}{cc} 4 \\ \times 8 \end{array}$$
$$\begin{array}{cc} 0 \\ \times 3 \end{array}$$
$$\begin{array}{cc} 5 \\ \times 3 \end{array}$$
$$\begin{array}{cc} 7 \\ \times 8 \end{array}$$
$$\begin{array}{cc} 6 \\ \times 6 \end{array}$$

H.
$$\begin{array}{cc} 4 \\ \times 0 \end{array}$$
$$\begin{array}{cc} 3 \\ \times 6 \end{array}$$
$$\begin{array}{cc} 2 \\ \times 2 \end{array}$$
$$\begin{array}{cc} 7 \\ \times 1 \end{array}$$
$$\begin{array}{cc} 0 \\ \times 5 \end{array}$$
$$\begin{array}{cc} 9 \\ \times 7 \end{array}$$
$$\begin{array}{cc} 4 \\ \times 4 \end{array}$$
$$\begin{array}{cc} 1 \\ \times 9 \end{array}$$
$$\begin{array}{cc} 3 \\ \times 1 \end{array}$$
$$\begin{array}{cc} 8 \\ \times 7 \end{array}$$

I.
$$\begin{array}{cc} 2 \\ \times 6 \end{array}$$
$$\begin{array}{cc} 7 \\ \times 4 \end{array}$$
$$\begin{array}{cc} 5 \\ \times 5 \end{array}$$
$$\begin{array}{cc} 0 \\ \times 0 \end{array}$$
$$\begin{array}{cc} 8 \\ \times 4 \end{array}$$
$$\begin{array}{cc} 5 \\ \times 8 \end{array}$$
$$\begin{array}{cc} 1 \\ \times 0 \end{array}$$
$$\begin{array}{cc} 8 \\ \times 1 \end{array}$$
$$\begin{array}{cc} 6 \\ \times 0 \end{array}$$
$$\begin{array}{cc} 9 \\ \times 2 \end{array}$$

J.
$$\begin{array}{cc} 6 \\ \times 5 \end{array}$$
$$\begin{array}{cc} 1 \\ \times 4 \end{array}$$
$$\begin{array}{cc} 5 \\ \times 2 \end{array}$$
$$\begin{array}{cc} 4 \\ \times 9 \end{array}$$
$$\begin{array}{cc} 7 \\ \times 7 \end{array}$$
$$\begin{array}{cc} 2 \\ \times 9 \end{array}$$
$$\begin{array}{cc} 7 \\ \times 0 \end{array}$$
$$\begin{array}{cc} 6 \\ \times 9 \end{array}$$
$$\begin{array}{cc} 3 \\ \times 0 \end{array}$$
$$\begin{array}{cc} 4 \\ \times 7 \end{array}$$

Minutes

1	2	3	4	5

Score

A.
$$\begin{array}{ccccccccc} 3 & 7 & 1 & 6 & 0 & 5 & 9 & 2 & 7 & 4 \\ \times 6 & \times 2 & \times 3 & \times 7 & \times 9 & \times 4 & \times 1 & \times 6 & \times 9 & \times 5 \end{array}$$

B.
$$\begin{array}{ccccccccc} 8 & 1 & 7 & 2 & 6 & 4 & 3 & 8 & 0 & 5 \\ \times 1 & \times 5 & \times 0 & \times 2 & \times 0 & \times 8 & \times 2 & \times 7 & \times 3 & \times 9 \end{array}$$

C.
$$\begin{array}{ccccccccc} 5 & 9 & 4 & 0 & 6 & 0 & 7 & 4 & 5 & 2 \\ \times 1 & \times 3 & \times 2 & \times 8 & \times 5 & \times 1 & \times 8 & \times 4 & \times 3 & \times 0 \end{array}$$

D.
$$\begin{array}{ccccccccc} 7 & 2 & 9 & 2 & 8 & 1 & 5 & 0 & 7 & 3 \\ \times 6 & \times 5 & \times 2 & \times 8 & \times 4 & \times 2 & \times 8 & \times 4 & \times 4 & \times 8 \end{array}$$

E.
$$\begin{array}{ccccccccc} 6 & 1 & 3 & 8 & 2 & 7 & 3 & 6 & 1 & 6 \\ \times 6 & \times 0 & \times 7 & \times 6 & \times 3 & \times 1 & \times 5 & \times 9 & \times 8 & \times 4 \end{array}$$

F.
$$\begin{array}{ccccccccc} 1 & 8 & 4 & 3 & 5 & 4 & 6 & 1 & 9 & 2 \\ \times 6 & \times 8 & \times 7 & \times 1 & \times 2 & \times 0 & \times 2 & \times 4 & \times 0 & \times 7 \end{array}$$

G.
$$\begin{array}{ccccccccc} 5 & 0 & 8 & 2 & 9 & 0 & 4 & 5 & 3 & 8 \\ \times 5 & \times 7 & \times 3 & \times 1 & \times 6 & \times 2 & \times 3 & \times 7 & \times 3 & \times 9 \end{array}$$

H.
$$\begin{array}{ccccccccc} 9 & 4 & 8 & 1 & 4 & 5 & 3 & 9 & 2 & 7 \\ \times 8 & \times 1 & \times 0 & \times 7 & \times 6 & \times 0 & \times 9 & \times 5 & \times 4 & \times 7 \end{array}$$

I.
$$\begin{array}{ccccccccc} 0 & 6 & 3 & 7 & 1 & 8 & 0 & 9 & 6 & 8 \\ \times 0 & \times 8 & \times 0 & \times 3 & \times 1 & \times 5 & \times 6 & \times 7 & \times 1 & \times 2 \end{array}$$

J.
$$\begin{array}{ccccccccc} 6 & 5 & 2 & 9 & 0 & 9 & 4 & 3 & 7 & 1 \\ \times 3 & \times 6 & \times 9 & \times 4 & \times 5 & \times 9 & \times 9 & \times 4 & \times 5 & \times 9 \end{array}$$

Minutes

1	2	3	4	5

Score

Name_____

A.
$$\begin{array}{c}7\\ \times 4\end{array} \quad \begin{array}{c}4\\ \times 6\end{array} \quad \begin{array}{c}3\\ \times 1\end{array} \quad \begin{array}{c}9\\ \times 5\end{array} \quad \begin{array}{c}1\\ \times 4\end{array} \quad \begin{array}{c}8\\ \times 4\end{array} \quad \begin{array}{c}2\\ \times 3\end{array} \quad \begin{array}{c}6\\ \times 8\end{array} \quad \begin{array}{c}0\\ \times 6\end{array} \quad \begin{array}{c}5\\ \times 5\end{array}$$

B.
$$\begin{array}{c}8\\ \times 1\end{array} \quad \begin{array}{c}4\\ \times 0\end{array} \quad \begin{array}{c}0\\ \times 3\end{array} \quad \begin{array}{c}4\\ \times 3\end{array} \quad \begin{array}{c}3\\ \times 5\end{array} \quad \begin{array}{c}6\\ \times 3\end{array} \quad \begin{array}{c}7\\ \times 3\end{array} \quad \begin{array}{c}1\\ \times 0\end{array} \quad \begin{array}{c}8\\ \times 9\end{array} \quad \begin{array}{c}2\\ \times 7\end{array}$$

C.
$$\begin{array}{c}5\\ \times 4\end{array} \quad \begin{array}{c}2\\ \times 0\end{array} \quad \begin{array}{c}8\\ \times 7\end{array} \quad \begin{array}{c}0\\ \times 0\end{array} \quad \begin{array}{c}5\\ \times 1\end{array} \quad \begin{array}{c}4\\ \times 7\end{array} \quad \begin{array}{c}1\\ \times 6\end{array} \quad \begin{array}{c}9\\ \times 1\end{array} \quad \begin{array}{c}3\\ \times 8\end{array} \quad \begin{array}{c}6\\ \times 0\end{array}$$

D.
$$\begin{array}{c}7\\ \times 1\end{array} \quad \begin{array}{c}4\\ \times 9\end{array} \quad \begin{array}{c}2\\ \times 4\end{array} \quad \begin{array}{c}6\\ \times 7\end{array} \quad \begin{array}{c}9\\ \times 0\end{array} \quad \begin{array}{c}0\\ \times 7\end{array} \quad \begin{array}{c}5\\ \times 9\end{array} \quad \begin{array}{c}7\\ \times 6\end{array} \quad \begin{array}{c}1\\ \times 3\end{array} \quad \begin{array}{c}3\\ \times 4\end{array}$$

E.
$$\begin{array}{c}0\\ \times 9\end{array} \quad \begin{array}{c}8\\ \times 5\end{array} \quad \begin{array}{c}3\\ \times 2\end{array} \quad \begin{array}{c}5\\ \times 6\end{array} \quad \begin{array}{c}1\\ \times 1\end{array} \quad \begin{array}{c}9\\ \times 4\end{array} \quad \begin{array}{c}5\\ \times 0\end{array} \quad \begin{array}{c}2\\ \times 2\end{array} \quad \begin{array}{c}6\\ \times 2\end{array} \quad \begin{array}{c}4\\ \times 5\end{array}$$

F.
$$\begin{array}{c}7\\ \times 7\end{array} \quad \begin{array}{c}3\\ \times 9\end{array} \quad \begin{array}{c}1\\ \times 5\end{array} \quad \begin{array}{c}8\\ \times 0\end{array} \quad \begin{array}{c}6\\ \times 6\end{array} \quad \begin{array}{c}4\\ \times 1\end{array} \quad \begin{array}{c}2\\ \times 6\end{array} \quad \begin{array}{c}8\\ \times 3\end{array} \quad \begin{array}{c}0\\ \times 2\end{array} \quad \begin{array}{c}5\\ \times 2\end{array}$$

G.
$$\begin{array}{c}9\\ \times 3\end{array} \quad \begin{array}{c}1\\ \times 9\end{array} \quad \begin{array}{c}7\\ \times 0\end{array} \quad \begin{array}{c}4\\ \times 4\end{array} \quad \begin{array}{c}0\\ \times 5\end{array} \quad \begin{array}{c}5\\ \times 8\end{array} \quad \begin{array}{c}9\\ \times 9\end{array} \quad \begin{array}{c}2\\ \times 1\end{array} \quad \begin{array}{c}8\\ \times 8\end{array} \quad \begin{array}{c}3\\ \times 0\end{array}$$

H.
$$\begin{array}{c}2\\ \times 8\end{array} \quad \begin{array}{c}6\\ \times 1\end{array} \quad \begin{array}{c}6\\ \times 9\end{array} \quad \begin{array}{c}1\\ \times 7\end{array} \quad \begin{array}{c}7\\ \times 5\end{array} \quad \begin{array}{c}4\\ \times 8\end{array} \quad \begin{array}{c}0\\ \times 1\end{array} \quad \begin{array}{c}9\\ \times 8\end{array} \quad \begin{array}{c}3\\ \times 7\end{array} \quad \begin{array}{c}7\\ \times 9\end{array}$$

I.
$$\begin{array}{c}5\\ \times 7\end{array} \quad \begin{array}{c}0\\ \times 8\end{array} \quad \begin{array}{c}6\\ \times 4\end{array} \quad \begin{array}{c}3\\ \times 3\end{array} \quad \begin{array}{c}5\\ \times 3\end{array} \quad \begin{array}{c}2\\ \times 9\end{array} \quad \begin{array}{c}8\\ \times 6\end{array} \quad \begin{array}{c}7\\ \times 2\end{array} \quad \begin{array}{c}1\\ \times 2\end{array} \quad \begin{array}{c}9\\ \times 7\end{array}$$

J.
$$\begin{array}{c}8\\ \times 2\end{array} \quad \begin{array}{c}3\\ \times 6\end{array} \quad \begin{array}{c}0\\ \times 4\end{array} \quad \begin{array}{c}7\\ \times 8\end{array} \quad \begin{array}{c}2\\ \times 5\end{array} \quad \begin{array}{c}9\\ \times 2\end{array} \quad \begin{array}{c}1\\ \times 8\end{array} \quad \begin{array}{c}9\\ \times 6\end{array} \quad \begin{array}{c}4\\ \times 2\end{array} \quad \begin{array}{c}6\\ \times 5\end{array}$$

Minutes

1	2	3	4	5

Score

A.	9 x 1 =	5 x 8 =	2 x 5 =	7 x 5 =	4 x 7 =
B.	0 x 5 =	8 x 0 =	8 x 6 =	0 x 9 =	6 x 3 =
C.	9 x 6 =	7 x 4 =	7 x 0 =	4 x 4 =	0 x 3 =
D.	6 x 4 =	1 x 7 =	3 x 7 =	3 x 1 =	5 x 3 =
E.	9 x 9 =	9 x 3 =	0 x 4 =	7 x 9 =	6 x 0 =
F.	1 x 3 =	4 x 8 =	5 x 7 =	5 x 2 =	2 x 1 =
G.	9 x 4 =	1 x 0 =	7 x 1 =	0 x 0 =	3 x 6 =
H.	4 x 3 =	7 x 8 =	2 x 4 =	8 x 5 =	1 x 2 =
I.	3 x 8 =	9 x 8 =	5 x 1 =	3 x 0 =	7 x 3 =
J.	8 x 1 =	5 x 6 =	2 x 0 =	6 x 2 =	0 x 8 =
K.	9 x 7 =	0 x 1 =	6 x 6 =	1 x 6 =	2 x 9 =
L.	5 x 0 =	6 x 9 =	3 x 2 =	8 x 9 =	4 x 0 =
M.	7 x 2 =	2 x 6 =	0 x 7 =	3 x 5 =	4 x 6 =
N.	2 x 3 =	5 x 9 =	4 x 2 =	1 x 1 =	7 x 7 =
O.	6 x 5 =	0 x 6 =	5 x 5 =	9 x 2 =	8 x 2 =
P.	3 x 9 =	6 x 1 =	1 x 5 =	2 x 8 =	2 x 2 =
Q.	1 x 4 =	1 x 9 =	4 x 9 =	0 x 2 =	6 x 7 =
R.	8 x 4 =	4 x 5 =	7 x 6 =	9 x 5 =	5 x 4 =
S.	8 x 8 =	6 x 8 =	9 x 0 =	3 x 3 =	8 x 7 =
T.	3 x 4 =	4 x 1 =	2 x 7 =	8 x 3 =	1 x 8 =

Minutes   **Score**

1	2	3	4	5	

Name_____   **Multiplication Facts:** 0 to 9

A.	7 x 6 =	4 x 6 =	2 x 5 =	0 x 8 =	5 x 7 =
B.	1 x 5 =	8 x 9 =	8 x 2 =	7 x 1 =	2 x 4 =
C.	6 x 7 =	0 x 4 =	6 x 1 =	4 x 9 =	9 x 2 =
D.	5 x 6 =	6 x 3 =	2 x 0 =	3 x 8 =	0 x 7 =
E.	9 x 6 =	4 x 2 =	9 x 9 =	5 x 0 =	3 x 3 =
F.	1 x 2 =	7 x 5 =	2 x 9 =	1 x 3 =	4 x 5 =
G.	6 x 0 =	3 x 7 =	0 x 1 =	7 x 9 =	1 x 9 =
H.	3 x 4 =	4 x 8 =	6 x 6 =	2 x 3 =	5 x 5 =
I.	2 x 8 =	7 x 0 =	8 x 5 =	4 x 1 =	7 x 4 =
J.	9 x 0 =	1 x 1 =	3 x 2 =	6 x 9 =	6 x 2 =
K.	8 x 6 =	8 x 1 =	5 x 1 =	0 x 3 =	1 x 4 =
L.	5 x 3 =	2 x 2 =	4 x 0 =	4 x 4 =	8 x 8 =
M.	0 x 0 =	8 x 4 =	6 x 5 =	2 x 7 =	3 x 6 =
N.	9 x 5 =	3 x 1 =	0 x 6 =	7 x 8 =	1 x 8 =
O.	3 x 9 =	7 x 2 =	8 x 0 =	2 x 1 =	0 x 2 =
P.	9 x 8 =	1 x 0 =	9 x 1 =	5 x 9 =	7 x 3 =
Q.	6 x 4 =	9 x 7 =	1 x 7 =	9 x 3 =	5 x 4 =
R.	7 x 7 =	0 x 5 =	5 x 8 =	3 x 0 =	6 x 8 =
S.	9 x 4 =	4 x 3 =	8 x 7 =	0 x 9 =	3 x 5 =
T.	1 x 6 =	5 x 2 =	2 x 6 =	4 x 7 =	8 x 3 =

Minutes

1	2	3	4	5

Score

A.	5)5	3)6	3)15	1)0	2)6	1)3	4)8	2)4	2)8	4)20
B.	4)20	3)12	1)2	4)4	2)10	3)6	3)3	5)25	3)15	5)20
C.	2)4	5)15	1)1	5)5	3)0	2)2	4)20	1)4	4)16	2)0
D.	3)15	1)5	4)16	5)0	1)1	3)3	2)8	2)10	1)3	4)0
E.	5)20	3)0	1)2	4)12	5)10	4)16	3)9	5)25	2)8	5)15
F.	4)0	2)6	4)12	3)12	3)15	4)8	1)5	2)2	2)10	5)20
G.	5)5	4)16	5)25	3)3	1)0	1)2	3)9	1)3	4)0	5)15
H.	3)12	2)0	1)5	3)3	5)25	1)4	4)8	3)9	5)10	2)8
I.	3)12	5)5	2)6	2)4	4)4	3)6	5)0	2)2	5)15	2)10
J.	4)4	1)1	3)9	4)12	2)4	1)4	4)8	3)0	5)10	2)0

Minutes

1	2	3	4	5

Score

Name_____   **Division Facts: 0 to 5**

A.	4)4̄	3)1̄2̄	2)6̄	1)0̄	5)1̄0̄	4)8̄	2)2̄	3)9̄	4)1̄2̄	5)1̄5̄
B.	3)6̄	5)1̄0̄	1)1̄	1)3̄	3)3̄	2)6̄	4)2̄0̄	3)9̄	1)3̄	3)1̄2̄
C.	2)4̄	1)5̄	4)1̄2̄	4)4̄	4)1̄6̄	5)2̄5̄	2)6̄	2)1̄0̄	5)1̄5̄	3)0̄
D.	2)8̄	5)2̄0̄	5)1̄5̄	4)1̄2̄	2)2̄	1)3̄	5)0̄	3)1̄5̄	1)1̄	4)1̄6̄
E.	4)2̄0̄	1)4̄	4)0̄	3)3̄	1)2̄	3)1̄5̄	4)4̄	5)5̄	3)9̄	2)1̄0̄
F.	5)1̄0̄	4)2̄0̄	4)8̄	5)2̄0̄	2)4̄	1)0̄	2)6̄	5)1̄5̄	2)0̄	4)1̄6̄
G.	4)8̄	3)0̄	1)4̄	5)2̄5̄	2)0̄	4)1̄6̄	3)6̄	5)5̄	1)4̄	4)4̄
H.	5)1̄0̄	2)4̄	1)2̄	3)1̄2̄	5)5̄	2)8̄	4)2̄0̄	3)1̄5̄	5)2̄0̄	2)2̄
I.	5)2̄5̄	5)5̄	3)1̄2̄	3)6̄	1)2̄	1)1̄	4)0̄	2)1̄0̄	5)2̄5̄	1)5̄
J.	3)3̄	5)0̄	2)1̄0̄	2)2̄	4)1̄2̄	4)8̄	2)8̄	1)5̄	3)6̄	5)2̄0̄

Minutes

1	2	3	4	5

Score

A.	$1\overline{)4}$	$6\overline{)6}$	$5\overline{)35}$	$2\overline{)12}$	$5\overline{)10}$	$3\overline{)6}$	$3\overline{)12}$	$7\overline{)21}$	$6\overline{)12}$	$2\overline{)2}$
B.	$5\overline{)35}$	$7\overline{)28}$	$3\overline{)3}$	$3\overline{)15}$	$5\overline{)0}$	$4\overline{)16}$	$6\overline{)36}$	$5\overline{)20}$	$1\overline{)7}$	$4\overline{)24}$
C.	$4\overline{)12}$	$6\overline{)24}$	$2\overline{)6}$	$7\overline{)42}$	$4\overline{)28}$	$3\overline{)21}$	$4\overline{)4}$	$2\overline{)0}$	$7\overline{)14}$	$1\overline{)1}$
D.	$2\overline{)4}$	$1\overline{)0}$	$4\overline{)12}$	$2\overline{)4}$	$6\overline{)30}$	$7\overline{)28}$	$4\overline{)4}$	$5\overline{)25}$	$5\overline{)10}$	$6\overline{)24}$
E.	$4\overline{)24}$	$5\overline{)15}$	$3\overline{)12}$	$7\overline{)7}$	$6\overline{)18}$	$1\overline{)3}$	$4\overline{)20}$	$5\overline{)30}$	$2\overline{)8}$	$7\overline{)0}$
F.	$2\overline{)14}$	$7\overline{)21}$	$6\overline{)12}$	$1\overline{)6}$	$3\overline{)9}$	$2\overline{)14}$	$4\overline{)0}$	$7\overline{)49}$	$3\overline{)18}$	$2\overline{)2}$
G.	$6\overline{)0}$	$3\overline{)18}$	$4\overline{)8}$	$2\overline{)10}$	$7\overline{)49}$	$5\overline{)15}$	$4\overline{)20}$	$5\overline{)5}$	$7\overline{)35}$	$1\overline{)6}$
H.	$7\overline{)42}$	$3\overline{)15}$	$1\overline{)5}$	$6\overline{)30}$	$7\overline{)7}$	$4\overline{)28}$	$6\overline{)6}$	$7\overline{)14}$	$3\overline{)3}$	$2\overline{)10}$
I.	$6\overline{)42}$	$2\overline{)6}$	$5\overline{)25}$	$5\overline{)5}$	$3\overline{)0}$	$1\overline{)7}$	$1\overline{)2}$	$4\overline{)16}$	$3\overline{)21}$	$5\overline{)30}$
J.	$1\overline{)5}$	$7\overline{)35}$	$2\overline{)12}$	$3\overline{)6}$	$4\overline{)8}$	$5\overline{)20}$	$2\overline{)8}$	$6\overline{)18}$	$3\overline{)9}$	$6\overline{)36}$

Minutes

1	2	3	4	5

Score

A.	$4\overline{)8}$	$7\overline{)49}$	$3\overline{)18}$	$5\overline{)15}$	$1\overline{)5}$	$6\overline{)24}$	$5\overline{)35}$	$1\overline{)4}$	$7\overline{)21}$	$3\overline{)6}$
B.	$6\overline{)18}$	$2\overline{)8}$	$7\overline{)7}$	$4\overline{)24}$	$6\overline{)36}$	$1\overline{)1}$	$5\overline{)10}$	$7\overline{)35}$	$3\overline{)15}$	$4\overline{)16}$
C.	$1\overline{)6}$	$5\overline{)5}$	$4\overline{)12}$	$7\overline{)0}$	$4\overline{)28}$	$5\overline{)30}$	$6\overline{)12}$	$3\overline{)3}$	$2\overline{)4}$	$6\overline{)30}$
D.	$4\overline{)16}$	$7\overline{)42}$	$3\overline{)6}$	$5\overline{)20}$	$2\overline{)12}$	$6\overline{)6}$	$2\overline{)6}$	$3\overline{)12}$	$7\overline{)28}$	$3\overline{)21}$
E.	$5\overline{)25}$	$1\overline{)6}$	$5\overline{)0}$	$6\overline{)36}$	$1\overline{)3}$	$3\overline{)9}$	$7\overline{)14}$	$4\overline{)4}$	$3\overline{)18}$	$6\overline{)42}$
F.	$2\overline{)2}$	$5\overline{)10}$	$7\overline{)21}$	$2\overline{)10}$	$4\overline{)20}$	$6\overline{)30}$	$3\overline{)3}$	$6\overline{)0}$	$4\overline{)12}$	$2\overline{)14}$
G.	$2\overline{)14}$	$5\overline{)30}$	$6\overline{)12}$	$4\overline{)0}$	$7\overline{)35}$	$1\overline{)7}$	$2\overline{)6}$	$5\overline{)15}$	$1\overline{)5}$	$7\overline{)49}$
H.	$6\overline{)24}$	$2\overline{)2}$	$3\overline{)12}$	$5\overline{)5}$	$1\overline{)2}$	$3\overline{)0}$	$6\overline{)18}$	$4\overline{)8}$	$7\overline{)7}$	$2\overline{)10}$
I.	$4\overline{)28}$	$6\overline{)6}$	$2\overline{)4}$	$5\overline{)25}$	$3\overline{)15}$	$7\overline{)28}$	$1\overline{)0}$	$4\overline{)20}$	$6\overline{)42}$	$3\overline{)21}$
J.	$5\overline{)35}$	$2\overline{)8}$	$7\overline{)14}$	$3\overline{)9}$	$4\overline{)4}$	$5\overline{)20}$	$2\overline{)12}$	$7\overline{)42}$	$2\overline{)0}$	$4\overline{)24}$

Minutes

1	2	3	4	5

Score

A.	$3\overline{)27}$	$4\overline{)12}$	$7\overline{)14}$	$2\overline{)8}$	$9\overline{)63}$	$3\overline{)6}$	$5\overline{)10}$	$3\overline{)9}$	$8\overline{)48}$	$3\overline{)15}$
B.	$1\overline{)3}$	$5\overline{)25}$	$7\overline{)0}$	$2\overline{)16}$	$6\overline{)36}$	$2\overline{)12}$	$4\overline{)24}$	$9\overline{)36}$	$3\overline{)24}$	$8\overline{)16}$
C.	$5\overline{)40}$	$1\overline{)7}$	$9\overline{)18}$	$2\overline{)2}$	$6\overline{)0}$	$9\overline{)81}$	$8\overline{)56}$	$4\overline{)4}$	$5\overline{)45}$	$6\overline{)18}$
D.	$3\overline{)9}$	$8\overline{)32}$	$1\overline{)0}$	$6\overline{)48}$	$4\overline{)16}$	$7\overline{)35}$	$1\overline{)6}$	$5\overline{)5}$	$9\overline{)0}$	$2\overline{)18}$
E.	$6\overline{)30}$	$2\overline{)10}$	$4\overline{)0}$	$8\overline{)72}$	$1\overline{)5}$	$9\overline{)54}$	$3\overline{)3}$	$5\overline{)20}$	$2\overline{)6}$	$7\overline{)49}$
F.	$4\overline{)36}$	$8\overline{)0}$	$7\overline{)14}$	$6\overline{)12}$	$7\overline{)63}$	$8\overline{)48}$	$7\overline{)7}$	$3\overline{)18}$	$9\overline{)81}$	$3\overline{)12}$
G.	$7\overline{)28}$	$2\overline{)16}$	$9\overline{)9}$	$1\overline{)5}$	$4\overline{)16}$	$5\overline{)0}$	$8\overline{)24}$	$1\overline{)2}$	$4\overline{)28}$	$6\overline{)42}$
H.	$5\overline{)15}$	$2\overline{)4}$	$7\overline{)42}$	$1\overline{)1}$	$8\overline{)8}$	$9\overline{)36}$	$4\overline{)32}$	$9\overline{)27}$	$5\overline{)30}$	$1\overline{)9}$
I.	$3\overline{)21}$	$9\overline{)45}$	$4\overline{)20}$	$7\overline{)56}$	$2\overline{)0}$	$8\overline{)64}$	$5\overline{)15}$	$6\overline{)54}$	$4\overline{)8}$	$6\overline{)24}$
J.	$6\overline{)6}$	$1\overline{)8}$	$5\overline{)35}$	$8\overline{)40}$	$6\overline{)30}$	$3\overline{)0}$	$9\overline{)72}$	$2\overline{)14}$	$7\overline{)21}$	$1\overline{)4}$

Minutes

1	2	3	4	5

Score

A.	$9\overline{)63}$	$6\overline{)24}$	$4\overline{)4}$	$9\overline{)18}$	$1\overline{)7}$	$8\overline{)32}$	$5\overline{)15}$	$3\overline{)12}$	$1\overline{)8}$	$2\overline{)16}$
B.	$8\overline{)64}$	$4\overline{)36}$	$1\overline{)2}$	$7\overline{)0}$	$5\overline{)30}$	$3\overline{)24}$	$3\overline{)18}$	$9\overline{)54}$	$2\overline{)6}$	$7\overline{)35}$
C.	$2\overline{)12}$	$5\overline{)20}$	$6\overline{)48}$	$8\overline{)8}$	$3\overline{)6}$	$7\overline{)56}$	$5\overline{)0}$	$1\overline{)1}$	$9\overline{)45}$	$4\overline{)16}$
D.	$8\overline{)24}$	$5\overline{)40}$	$2\overline{)2}$	$9\overline{)27}$	$6\overline{)42}$	$1\overline{)4}$	$7\overline{)14}$	$4\overline{)24}$	$9\overline{)9}$	$3\overline{)0}$
E.	$7\overline{)63}$	$3\overline{)15}$	$7\overline{)21}$	$6\overline{)18}$	$4\overline{)32}$	$8\overline{)0}$	$5\overline{)20}$	$2\overline{)4}$	$7\overline{)28}$	$1\overline{)6}$
F.	$3\overline{)21}$	$9\overline{)36}$	$1\overline{)0}$	$6\overline{)6}$	$5\overline{)35}$	$4\overline{)12}$	$9\overline{)72}$	$2\overline{)10}$	$6\overline{)12}$	$8\overline{)56}$
G.	$6\overline{)54}$	$4\overline{)0}$	$8\overline{)32}$	$3\overline{)3}$	$2\overline{)18}$	$8\overline{)40}$	$5\overline{)5}$	$7\overline{)49}$	$1\overline{)8}$	$6\overline{)12}$
H.	$4\overline{)20}$	$9\overline{)36}$	$2\overline{)8}$	$9\overline{)0}$	$6\overline{)30}$	$1\overline{)3}$	$8\overline{)48}$	$7\overline{)7}$	$3\overline{)9}$	$5\overline{)25}$
I.	$5\overline{)10}$	$4\overline{)28}$	$7\overline{)21}$	$1\overline{)9}$	$8\overline{)16}$	$4\overline{)28}$	$3\overline{)27}$	$6\overline{)36}$	$2\overline{)0}$	$9\overline{)81}$
J.	$7\overline{)42}$	$1\overline{)5}$	$3\overline{)24}$	$2\overline{)16}$	$5\overline{)45}$	$8\overline{)64}$	$2\overline{)14}$	$6\overline{)0}$	$8\overline{)72}$	$4\overline{)8}$

Minutes | 1 | 2 | 3 | 4 | 5   **Score**

A.	$6\overline{)18}$	$1\overline{)6}$	$9\overline{)36}$	$3\overline{)18}$	$9\overline{)72}$	$6\overline{)36}$	$2\overline{)2}$	$9\overline{)63}$	$4\overline{)24}$	$8\overline{)32}$
B.	$3\overline{)6}$	$5\overline{)30}$	$1\overline{)2}$	$8\overline{)56}$	$3\overline{)9}$	$2\overline{)10}$	$6\overline{)0}$	$5\overline{)45}$	$9\overline{)9}$	$4\overline{)8}$
C.	$3\overline{)0}$	$8\overline{)16}$	$7\overline{)56}$	$3\overline{)24}$	$5\overline{)15}$	$4\overline{)36}$	$1\overline{)1}$	$7\overline{)42}$	$2\overline{)8}$	$6\overline{)54}$
D.	$4\overline{)16}$	$5\overline{)20}$	$2\overline{)18}$	$7\overline{)7}$	$5\overline{)0}$	$1\overline{)7}$	$4\overline{)4}$	$9\overline{)27}$	$7\overline{)21}$	$2\overline{)0}$
E.	$6\overline{)42}$	$2\overline{)4}$	$6\overline{)36}$	$1\overline{)5}$	$5\overline{)25}$	$9\overline{)54}$	$3\overline{)15}$	$7\overline{)35}$	$6\overline{)12}$	$5\overline{)5}$
F.	$4\overline{)32}$	$7\overline{)28}$	$3\overline{)3}$	$6\overline{)30}$	$2\overline{)12}$	$5\overline{)40}$	$4\overline{)0}$	$6\overline{)30}$	$1\overline{)4}$	$8\overline{)48}$
G.	$9\overline{)18}$	$2\overline{)16}$	$9\overline{)0}$	$4\overline{)12}$	$6\overline{)6}$	$1\overline{)0}$	$8\overline{)24}$	$3\overline{)27}$	$7\overline{)49}$	$4\overline{)12}$
H.	$7\overline{)14}$	$5\overline{)10}$	$9\overline{)72}$	$1\overline{)9}$	$8\overline{)8}$	$6\overline{)48}$	$3\overline{)12}$	$8\overline{)56}$	$8\overline{)72}$	$4\overline{)20}$
I.	$1\overline{)3}$	$8\overline{)40}$	$6\overline{)24}$	$1\overline{)2}$	$5\overline{)20}$	$9\overline{)81}$	$2\overline{)14}$	$7\overline{)0}$	$3\overline{)6}$	$9\overline{)45}$
J.	$7\overline{)63}$	$3\overline{)21}$	$5\overline{)35}$	$2\overline{)6}$	$8\overline{)0}$	$4\overline{)28}$	$6\overline{)54}$	$1\overline{)8}$	$8\overline{)64}$	$7\overline{)42}$

Minutes | 1 | 2 | 3 | 4 | 5 | **Score** [ ]

© Carson-Dellosa Publ. CD-0902

A.	$5\overline{)10}$	$4\overline{)28}$	$2\overline{)4}$	$9\overline{)63}$	$6\overline{)30}$	$4\overline{)16}$	$9\overline{)0}$	$3\overline{)15}$	$8\overline{)72}$	$6\overline{)18}$
B.	$8\overline{)48}$	$3\overline{)6}$	$7\overline{)21}$	$1\overline{)3}$	$7\overline{)56}$	$6\overline{)0}$	$2\overline{)16}$	$6\overline{)54}$	$1\overline{)7}$	$9\overline{)45}$
C.	$7\overline{)49}$	$5\overline{)35}$	$3\overline{)24}$	$7\overline{)7}$	$3\overline{)12}$	$8\overline{)24}$	$1\overline{)1}$	$9\overline{)72}$	$7\overline{)35}$	$5\overline{)25}$
D.	$9\overline{)27}$	$1\overline{)0}$	$8\overline{)40}$	$5\overline{)15}$	$2\overline{)2}$	$6\overline{)48}$	$5\overline{)0}$	$4\overline{)24}$	$2\overline{)8}$	$5\overline{)15}$
E.	$7\overline{)49}$	$6\overline{)12}$	$3\overline{)3}$	$2\overline{)12}$	$9\overline{)9}$	$1\overline{)5}$	$6\overline{)24}$	$4\overline{)4}$	$8\overline{)64}$	$5\overline{)45}$
F.	$2\overline{)6}$	$6\overline{)24}$	$4\overline{)12}$	$3\overline{)0}$	$8\overline{)8}$	$4\overline{)36}$	$2\overline{)0}$	$7\overline{)28}$	$9\overline{)63}$	$3\overline{)21}$
G.	$6\overline{)42}$	$7\overline{)35}$	$1\overline{)8}$	$9\overline{)56}$	$3\overline{)27}$	$4\overline{)0}$	$5\overline{)5}$	$5\overline{)40}$	$1\overline{)4}$	$7\overline{)0}$
H.	$4\overline{)32}$	$2\overline{)18}$	$9\overline{)81}$	$8\overline{)54}$	$3\overline{)9}$	$1\overline{)3}$	$2\overline{)14}$	$9\overline{)36}$	$4\overline{)8}$	$8\overline{)16}$
I.	$7\overline{)14}$	$8\overline{)48}$	$5\overline{)20}$	$6\overline{)6}$	$1\overline{)2}$	$8\overline{)0}$	$5\overline{)30}$	$8\overline{)56}$	$1\overline{)9}$	$8\overline{)32}$
J.	$1\overline{)6}$	$6\overline{)54}$	$6\overline{)36}$	$3\overline{)18}$	$7\overline{)63}$	$4\overline{)8}$	$2\overline{)10}$	$7\overline{)42}$	$9\overline{)18}$	$4\overline{)20}$

Minutes

1	2	3	4	5

Score

A.	5)20	3)6	8)16	4)32	9)9	2)10	4)20	7)56	3)21	7)35
B.	8)72	6)18	2)6	7)0	5)45	4)24	8)8	1)5	7)49	6)36
C.	6)0	4)16	1)2	6)54	5)15	2)16	1)8	8)48	4)8	5)15
D.	3)9	7)14	6)30	3)18	4)0	9)63	1)1	9)45	5)30	2)2
E.	8)24	2)8	7)42	1)7	6)48	3)27	2)0	7)28	5)5	9)27
F.	2)14	8)64	4)28	5)40	1)6	3)3	4)32	6)12	3)15	8)40
G.	9)0	4)12	2)4	7)7	5)0	1)9	7)63	4)20	8)0	1)4
H.	1)3	9)81	6)24	5)10	8)64	7)49	3)24	9)18	6)42	8)32
I.	7)21	9)36	3)0	9)72	2)12	7)21	5)25	6)30	4)4	9)54
J.	5)35	2)18	9)27	8)32	4)36	6)6	1)0	3)12	5)40	8)56

Minutes

1	2	3	4	5

Score

A.	8)40	3)27	7)42	8)48	3)3	8)24	7)14	2)10	6)36	9)81
B.	6)42	4)32	1)4	9)45	5)10	3)15	5)40	4)4	1)3	9)27
C.	7)49	6)6	2)4	7)63	4)12	2)0	7)35	6)18	8)0	2)14
D.	1)0	9)72	3)24	4)0	7)7	6)54	1)8	9)18	4)28	5)20
E.	8)16	5)30	1)9	8)72	6)24	2)18	5)5	7)56	3)12	3)0
F.	2)12	9)0	4)20	3)6	6)36	7)0	2)2	8)56	1)6	7)28
G.	5)15	7)28	3)18	5)0	1)2	4)36	6)12	4)8	8)8	6)48
H.	8)48	1)5	7)49	4)32	5)40	6)0	2)16	6)18	9)63	2)8
I.	9)54	7)21	9)63	1)8	8)32	5)25	9)9	4)16	3)21	4)24
J.	5)35	3)9	9)36	8)64	5)45	2)6	5)25	1)1	6)30	4)16

Minutes

1	2	3	4	5

Score

A.	$36 \div 6 =$	$8 \div 1 =$	$45 \div 9 =$	$16 \div 8 =$	$35 \div 5 =$
B.	$24 \div 8 =$	$27 \div 9 =$	$20 \div 5 =$	$21 \div 3 =$	$8 \div 2 =$
C.	$20 \div 4 =$	$42 \div 7 =$	$18 \div 6 =$	$14 \div 2 =$	$28 \div 7 =$
D.	$56 \div 8 =$	$9 \div 3 =$	$3 \div 1 =$	$40 \div 8 =$	$12 \div 4 =$
E.	$10 \div 2 =$	$48 \div 6 =$	$45 \div 5 =$	$0 \div 6 =$	$15 \div 3 =$
F.	$7 \div 7 =$	$6 \div 2 =$	$18 \div 9 =$	$7 \div 1 =$	$32 \div 4 =$
G.	$5 \div 1 =$	$35 \div 5 =$	$56 \div 7 =$	$5 \div 5 =$	$30 \div 6 =$
H.	$18 \div 6 =$	$15 \div 5 =$	$18 \div 2 =$	$72 \div 8 =$	$2 \div 1 =$
I.	$30 \div 5 =$	$1 \div 1 =$	$21 \div 7 =$	$8 \div 4 =$	$0 \div 3 =$
J.	$9 \div 9 =$	$28 \div 4 =$	$16 \div 4 =$	$12 \div 2 =$	$36 \div 9 =$
K.	$8 \div 8 =$	$27 \div 3 =$	$6 \div 6 =$	$6 \div 3 =$	$0 \div 4 =$
L.	$12 \div 3 =$	$81 \div 9 =$	$0 \div 2 =$	$49 \div 7 =$	$36 \div 9 =$
M.	$30 \div 6 =$	$32 \div 8 =$	$9 \div 1 =$	$0 \div 8 =$	$14 \div 7 =$
N.	$35 \div 7 =$	$16 \div 2 =$	$0 \div 7 =$	$42 \div 6 =$	$6 \div 1 =$
O.	$45 \div 9 =$	$24 \div 4 =$	$10 \div 5 =$	$0 \div 1 =$	$12 \div 6 =$
P.	$2 \div 2 =$	$0 \div 5 =$	$24 \div 6 =$	$40 \div 5 =$	$24 \div 3 =$
Q.	$54 \div 6 =$	$27 \div 9 =$	$18 \div 3 =$	$25 \div 5 =$	$63 \div 9 =$
R.	$64 \div 8 =$	$4 \div 1 =$	$4 \div 4 =$	$0 \div 9 =$	$4 \div 2 =$
S.	$72 \div 8 =$	$63 \div 7 =$	$48 \div 8 =$	$72 \div 9 =$	$24 \div 8 =$
T.	$36 \div 4 =$	$54 \div 9 =$	$3 \div 3 =$	$40 \div 5 =$	$14 \div 7 =$

Minutes

1	2	3	4	5

Score

A.	$32 \div 8 =$	$64 \div 8 =$	$4 \div 2 =$	$36 \div 6 =$	$35 \div 5 =$
B.	$48 \div 6 =$	$9 \div 3 =$	$18 \div 6 =$	$16 \div 2 =$	$56 \div 7 =$
C.	$27 \div 9 =$	$63 \div 7 =$	$48 \div 8 =$	$9 \div 9 =$	$21 \div 3 =$
D.	$10 \div 2 =$	$36 \div 9 =$	$4 \div 1 =$	$24 \div 4 =$	$81 \div 9 =$
E.	$40 \div 5 =$	$42 \div 7 =$	$54 \div 6 =$	$2 \div 2 =$	$21 \div 7 =$
F.	$49 \div 7 =$	$6 \div 1 =$	$8 \div 4 =$	$7 \div 1 =$	$32 \div 4 =$
G.	$72 \div 8 =$	$12 \div 6 =$	$8 \div 1 =$	$12 \div 4 =$	$3 \div 1 =$
H.	$24 \div 3 =$	$20 \div 5 =$	$16 \div 8 =$	$0 \div 1 =$	$56 \div 7 =$
I.	$27 \div 9 =$	$32 \div 4 =$	$0 \div 3 =$	$63 \div 9 =$	$40 \div 8 =$
J.	$0 \div 7 =$	$1 \div 1 =$	$14 \div 7 =$	$6 \div 3 =$	$14 \div 2 =$
K.	$30 \div 6 =$	$12 \div 3 =$	$64 \div 8 =$	$49 \div 7 =$	$0 \div 6 =$
L.	$8 \div 8 =$	$42 \div 6 =$	$0 \div 2 =$	$5 \div 5 =$	$28 \div 4 =$
M.	$45 \div 9 =$	$35 \div 7 =$	$4 \div 4 =$	$8 \div 2 =$	$24 \div 8 =$
N.	$0 \div 4 =$	$12 \div 2 =$	$30 \div 5 =$	$12 \div 4 =$	$18 \div 3 =$
O.	$32 \div 8 =$	$6 \div 6 =$	$27 \div 3 =$	$0 \div 9 =$	$45 \div 5 =$
P.	$5 \div 1 =$	$15 \div 5 =$	$2 \div 1 =$	$3 \div 3 =$	$42 \div 6 =$
Q.	$7 \div 7 =$	$56 \div 8 =$	$18 \div 2 =$	$0 \div 5 =$	$7 \div 1 =$
R.	$72 \div 9 =$	$20 \div 4 =$	$0 \div 8 =$	$36 \div 4 =$	$36 \div 6 =$
S.	$25 \div 5 =$	$9 \div 1 =$	$28 \div 4 =$	$54 \div 9 =$	$28 \div 7 =$
T.	$15 \div 3 =$	$18 \div 9 =$	$24 \div 6 =$	$6 \div 2 =$	$45 \div 9 =$

Minutes

1	2	3	4	5

Score

A.   5   4   2   7   5   1
       x 0   x 1   x 6   5)25   x 3   4)28   x 7   3)3   x 7   7)28

B.   8   3   0   8   4
       2)14   x 2   x 2   7)21   x 6   x 8   5)10   x 2   9)81   9)36

C.   6   5   2   8   3   7
       4)32   x 3   x 9   3)0   2)12   x 1   x 0   8)48   x 5   x 9

D.   1   3   5   0   6   9
       6)42   x 4   x 0   7)0   x 3   6)24   x 2   x 5   x 3   5)5

E.   3   9   3   7   0   8
       2)2   x 6   x 7   x 1   6)30   1)0   x 7   x 9   3)6   x 5

F.   2   6   1   5   1
       x 0   5)5   4)12   x 0   x 1   1)7   9)18   x 4   8)24   x 9

G.   9   6   0   4   2   7
       x 1   x 6   x 4   9)72   2)4   x 4   5)45   7)42   x 8   x 0

H.   5   3   0
       3)24   x 2   8)32   x 3   5)0   1)6   x 8   3)12   8)40   x 9
                                                                          6

I.   7   9   2   4   1
       x 5   4)24   7)14   x 6   x 4   1)8   9)27   x 0   x 0   8)56

J.   1   9   9   8   0   4
       2)18   x 8   x 0   6)6   x 8   x 7   4)36   x 1   x 5   6)48

	Minutes					Score
	1	2	3	4	5	

Name_____ **Multiplication Facts:** 0 **to** 5

A.
$$2 \times 4$$ $$9 \times 0$$ $$1\overline{)5}$$ $$8\overline{)56}$$ $$1 \times 5$$ $$8 \times 0$$ $$8\overline{)72}$$ $$8\overline{)16}$$ $$3 \times 5$$ $$8 \times 7$$

B.
$$0 \times 0$$ $$7 \times 3$$ $$4 \times 9$$ $$6\overline{)0}$$ $$1 \times 0$$ $$6 \times 6$$ $$0 \times 4$$ $$8 \times 3$$ $$2\overline{)2}$$ $$9\overline{)27}$$

C.
$$6\overline{)54}$$ $$0 \times 1$$ $$3\overline{)9}$$ $$6\overline{)12}$$ $$3 \times 6$$ $$4 \times 1$$ $$5\overline{)30}$$ $$5 \times 2$$ $$2\overline{)12}$$ $$4 \times 7$$

D.
$$5 \times 8$$ $$5\overline{)35}$$ $$4 \times 0$$ $$9\overline{)45}$$ $$7 \times 4$$ $$2 \times 2$$ $$4\overline{)12}$$ $$9 \times 3$$ $$1 \times 6$$ $$3\overline{)6}$$

E.
$$1 \times 9$$ $$1\overline{)2}$$ $$2\overline{)18}$$ $$9 \times 7$$ $$0 \times 8$$ $$4\overline{)4}$$ $$3 \times 1$$ $$5\overline{)0}$$ $$8\overline{)64}$$ $$3 \times 8$$

F.
$$9 \times 5$$ $$1\overline{)7}$$ $$8 \times 2$$ $$2 \times 0$$ $$4\overline{)32}$$ $$6 \times 4$$ $$3\overline{)18}$$ $$2 \times 9$$ $$3\overline{)12}$$ $$7 \times 6$$

G.
$$2\overline{)8}$$ $$1 \times 3$$ $$7\overline{)21}$$ $$8 \times 5$$ $$7\overline{)7}$$ $$0 \times 2$$ $$7\overline{)42}$$ $$7\overline{)35}$$ $$4 \times 4$$ $$6\overline{)24}$$

H.
$$5 \times 0$$ $$9\overline{)63}$$ $$1 \times 8$$ $$5\overline{)10}$$ $$1\overline{)1}$$ $$7 \times 0$$ $$8\overline{)32}$$ $$5 \times 5$$ $$6 \times 9$$ $$7\overline{)49}$$

I.
$$3 \times 0$$ $$9\overline{)0}$$ $$6 \times 1$$ $$9\overline{)72}$$ $$0 \times 7$$ $$2\overline{)6}$$ $$9 \times 9$$ $$6 \times 0$$ $$6\overline{)48}$$ $$9 \times 1$$

J.
$$3 \times 3$$ $$3\overline{)0}$$ $$7 \times 2$$ $$5 \times 6$$ $$1\overline{)8}$$ $$6 \times 8$$ $$5\overline{)20}$$ $$5\overline{)35}$$ $$2 \times 7$$ $$4\overline{)36}$$

Minutes **Score**

1	2	3	4	5

Name _____

Grade _____

★ ★ ★ ★ ★ SCORE SHEET ★ ★ ★ ★ ★

Page	Factors/ Divisors	Time	0–69	70	71	72	73	74	75	76	77	78	79	80	81	82	83	84	85	86	87	88	89	90	91	92	93	94	95	96	97	98	99	100

Math Master

This certificate is
presented to

_____

for attaining
100% accuracy
within a _____ minute
time limit on the
Minute Math Tests!

Fast Facts Award
presented to

_____

who has demonstrated the ability
to think quickly and accurately
when working _____ problems.

Date _____

Signature_____

Multiply to solve the problems. Then circle the correct bases at the bottom of the page.

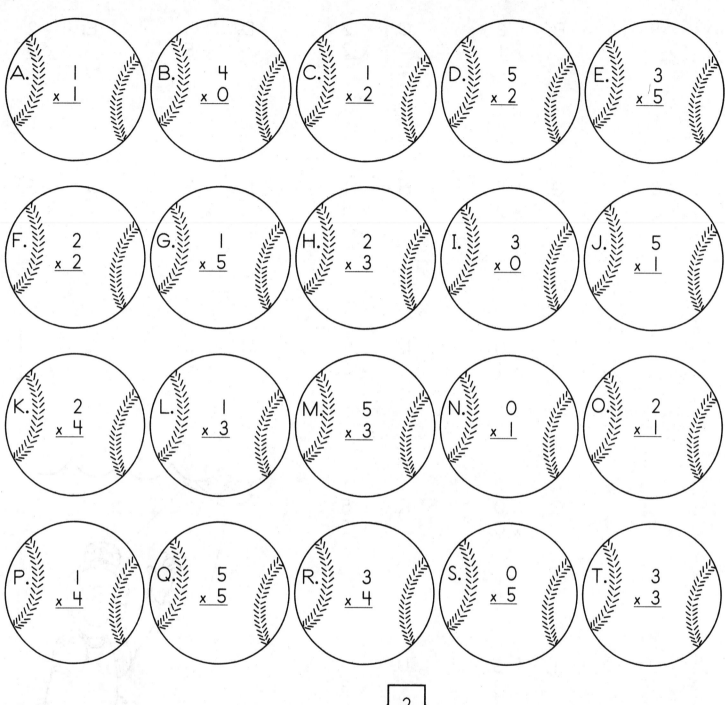

A.
$$1 \times 1$$

B.
$$4 \times 0$$

C.
$$1 \times 2$$

D.
$$5 \times 2$$

E.
$$3 \times 5$$

F.
$$2 \times 2$$

G.
$$1 \times 5$$

H.
$$2 \times 3$$

I.
$$3 \times 0$$

J.
$$5 \times 1$$

K.
$$2 \times 4$$

L.
$$1 \times 3$$

M.
$$5 \times 3$$

N.
$$0 \times 1$$

O.
$$2 \times 1$$

P.
$$1 \times 4$$

Q.
$$5 \times 5$$

R.
$$3 \times 4$$

S.
$$0 \times 5$$

T.
$$3 \times 3$$

Rules of the game:

- 1 row complete, circle first base
- 2 rows complete, circle second base
- 3 rows complete, circle third base
- 4 rows complete, circle Home Run!

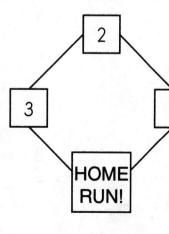

Name_____

Multiply to solve the problems.

A.   4
  x 3
	B. 3
	  x 1
		C. 2
		  x 2
			D. 5
			  x 5
				E. 2
				  x 0

F.   0
  x 3
	G. 4
	  x 2
		H. 1
		  x 5
			I. 5
			  x 4
				J. 5
				  x 0

K.   2
  x 5
	L. 0
	  x 1
		M. 2
		  x 3
			N. 3
			  x 4
				O. 4
				  x 1

P.   4
  x 4
	Q. 0
	  x 0
		R. 5
		  x 2

S.   2
  x 1
	T. 5
	  x 3
		U. 3
		  x 3

V.   1
  x 0
	W. 4
	  x 0
		X. 3
		  x 5

Multiply or divide to solve the problems. Then color in the flavors using the answer key.

Color Key

0 = red	1 = green	2 = yellow	4 = orange	5 = blue

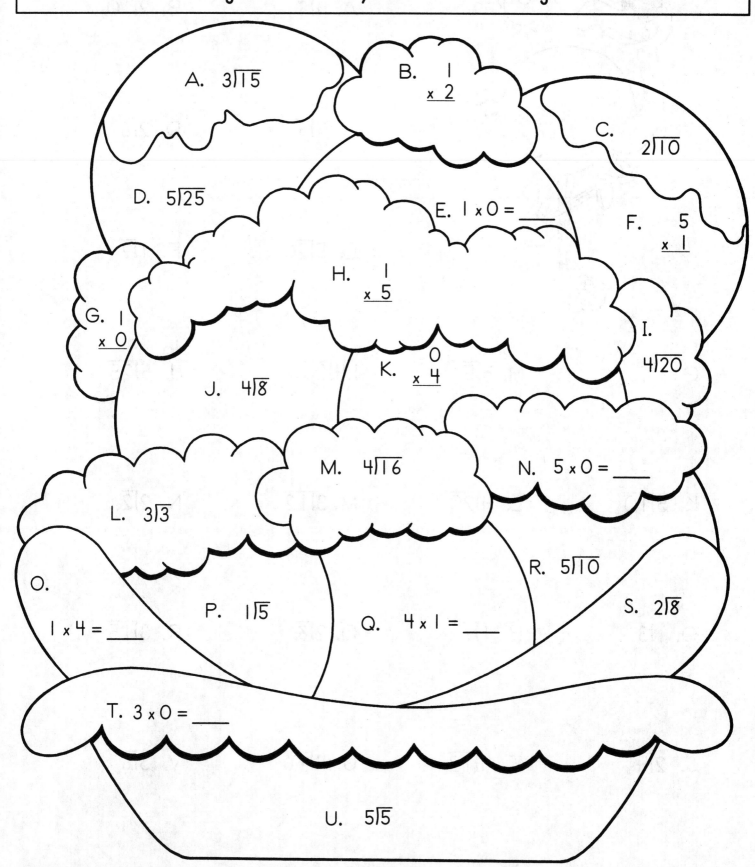

A. $3\overline{)15}$

B. $\begin{array}{r} 1 \\ \times\ 2 \\ \hline \end{array}$

C. $2\overline{)10}$

D. $5\overline{)25}$

E. $1 \times 0 = \underline{\ \ \ }$

F. $\begin{array}{r} 5 \\ \times\ 1 \\ \hline \end{array}$

G. $\begin{array}{r} 1 \\ \times\ 0 \\ \hline \end{array}$

H. $\begin{array}{r} 1 \\ \times\ 5 \\ \hline \end{array}$

I. $4\overline{)20}$

J. $4\overline{)8}$

K. $\begin{array}{r} 0 \\ \times\ 4 \\ \hline \end{array}$

L. $3\overline{)3}$

M. $4\overline{)16}$

N. $5 \times 0 = \underline{\ \ \ }$

O. $1 \times 4 = \underline{\ \ \ }$

P. $1\overline{)5}$

Q. $4 \times 1 = \underline{\ \ \ }$

R. $5\overline{)10}$

S. $2\overline{)8}$

T. $3 \times 0 = \underline{\ \ \ }$

U. $5\overline{)5}$

Name_____

Divide to solve the problems.

A. 4⟌8

B. 2⟌10

C. 4⟌4

D. 2⟌6

E. 5⟌20

F. 1⟌2

G. 1⟌0

H. 5⟌5

I. 4⟌20

J. 5⟌25

K. 5⟌10

L. 4⟌20

M. 3⟌12

N. 2⟌2

O. 1⟌3

P. 1⟌1

Q. 2⟌8

R. 3⟌15

S. 2⟌4

T. 4⟌12

U. 4⟌16

V. 3⟌6

Name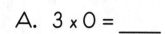_____

Multiply or divide to solve the problems.

A. $3 \times 0 =$ ____

B. $2 \div 1 =$ ____

C. $1 \times 1 =$ ____

D. $2 \times 2 =$ ____

E. $9 \div 3 =$ ____

F. $5 \div 1 =$ ____

G. $16 \div 4 =$ ____

H. $4 \div 1 =$ ____

I. $1 \times 4 =$ ____

J. $25 \div 5 =$ ____

K. $20 \div 4 =$ ____

L. $1 \times 3 =$ ____

M. $8 \div 2 =$ ____

N. $5 \times 1 =$ ____

O. $10 \div 2 =$ ____

P. $20 \div 5 =$ ____

Q. $15 \div 3 =$ ____

R. $12 \div 4 =$ ____

S. $4 \times 1 =$ ____

T. $5 \div 1 =$ ____

U. $1 \times 0 =$ ____

Name_____

Draw a line from each cupcake to the candle with the correct answer.

A.
0 x 5 =

8

G.
3 x 4 =

6

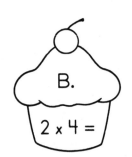
B.
2 x 4 =

0

H.
2 x 2 =

4

C.
3 x 3 =

5

I.
3 x 2 =

12

D.
1 x 5 =

9

J.
4 x 0 =

0

E.
5 x 5 =

25

K.
5 x 2 =

20

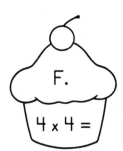
F.
4 x 4 =

16

L.
4 x 5 =

10

Multiply to solve the problems in the problem list. Use x and = to find the same problems hidden across or down in the puzzle. Then, circle each hidden problem and answer.

Problem List

1 x 4 = ____

5 x 3 = ____

3 x 4 = ____

0 x 3 = ____

4 x 4 = ____

2 x 4 = ____

1 x 2 = ____

5 x 5 = ____

3 x 3 = ____

0 x 1 = ____

4 x 5 = ____

2 x 2 = ____

1 x 1 = ____

5 x 2 = ____

3 x 2 = ____

4 x 2 = ____

4 x 1 = ____

2 x 1 = ____

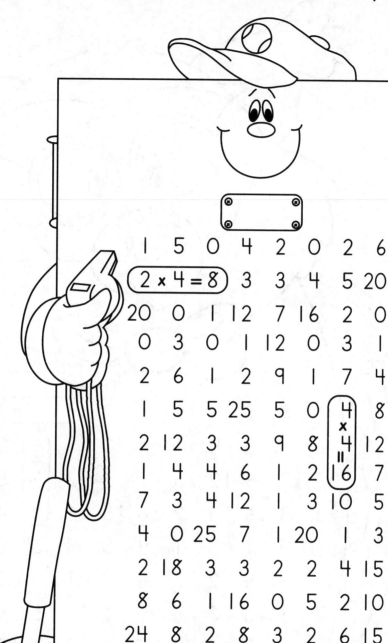

1	5	0	4	2	0	2	6
2 x 4 = 8			3	3	4	5	20
20	0	1	12	7	16	2	0
0	3	0	1	12	0	3	1
2	6	1	2	9	1	7	4
1	5	5	25	5	0	4	8
2	12	3	3	9	8	x 4 =	12
1	4	4	6	1	2	16	7
7	3	4	12	1	3	10	5
4	0	25	7	1	20	1	3
2	18	3	3	2	2	4	15
8	6	1	16	0	5	2	10
24	8	2	8	3	2	6	15
0	10	2	4	1	4	15	9

Divide to solve the problems in the problem list. Use ÷ and = to find the same problems hidden across and down in the puzzle. Then, circle each hidden problem and answer.

Problem List

3 ÷ 3 = ____
15 ÷ 5 = ____
20 ÷ 5 = ____
25 ÷ 5 = ____
10 ÷ 2 = ____
8 ÷ 4 = ____
9 ÷ 3 = ____
20 ÷ 4 = ____
15 ÷ 3 = ____
4 ÷ 2 = ____
12 ÷ 3 = ____
12 ÷ 4 = ____
5 ÷ 5 = ____
10 ÷ 5 = ____
8 ÷ 2 = ____
6 ÷ 3 = ____
16 ÷ 4 = ____
6 ÷ 2 = ____

1	8	2	4	15	8	12	4 ÷ 2 = 2	3
6	1	3	4	10	4	20	9	6	0	7
12	12	4	12	5	1	1	2	÷	5	2
3	3	16	4	2	16	15	6	2	8	6
6	4	1	3	1	4	5	9	=	3	1
16	8	4	2	3	4	3	1	3	0	5
7	1	15	3	5	20	2	20	5	4	0
16	5	2	25	5	5	7	1	20
6	3	2	7	9	2	3	5	9
1	5	1	10	2	5	3	2	1
12	3	10	4	8	1	6
2	5	5	1	6	25	8

36

Name_____

Multiply to solve the problems.

A.
3 x 4 = ___

B.
1 x 3 = ___

C.
5 x 5 = ___

D.
2 x 4 = ___

E.
4 x 1 = ___

F.
3 x 2 = ___

G.
1 x 0 = ___

H.
2 x 7 = ___

I.
2 x 5 = ___

J.
0 x 3 = ___

K.
4 x 5 = ___

L.
2 x 1 = ___

M.
3 x 5 = ___

N.
2 x 3 = ___

O.
4 x 0 = ___

P.
4 x 3 = ___

Q.
3 x 3 = ___

R.
7 x 3 = ___

S.
6 x 4 = ___

T.
5 x 2 = ___

U.
5 x 4 = ___

V.
6 x 3 = ___

W.
6 x 5 = ___

X.
4 x 6 = ___

Y.
3 x 6 = ___

Z.
6 x 6 = ___

Multiply to solve the problems. Circle the largest answer on the page to find out which truck will win the race.

A. 7
x 0

B. 6
x 1

C. 4
x 1

D. 3
x 2

E. 5
x 0

F. 6
x 0

G. 1
x 6

H. 3
x 5

I. 2
x 7

J. 6
x 2

K. 4
x 4

L. 5
x 7

M. 6
x 4

N. 3
x 3

O. 2
x 4

P. 4
x 5

Q. 6
x 3

R. 4
x 6

S. 7
x 2

T. 5
x 6

U. 7
x 1

V. 2
x 6

W. 4
x 3

X. 5
x 4

Divide to solve the problems. Help the hiker find his way to the cabin.

A. $1\overline{)4}$ B. $6\overline{)6}$

C. $2\overline{)12}$

G. $5\overline{)35}$ F. $5\overline{)20}$ E. $7\overline{)21}$ D. $3\overline{)6}$

H. $4\overline{)28}$

I. $7\overline{)42}$ J. $6\overline{)24}$ K. $5\overline{)15}$ L. $2\overline{)14}$

M. $7\overline{)14}$

Q. $1\overline{)7}$ P. $3\overline{)3}$ O. $6\overline{)36}$ N. $3\overline{)21}$

R. $6\overline{)30}$

S. $7\overline{)49}$ T. $3\overline{)18}$

Name_____

Multiply to solve the problems.

A. 6 x 2 = _____

B. 7 x 5 = _____

C. 7 x 3 = _____

D. 2 x 0 = _____

E. 7 x 6 = _____

F. 3 x 5 = _____

G. 0 x 0 = _____

H. 0 x 4 = _____

I. 3 x 4 = _____

J. 2 x 5 = _____

K. 4 x 5 = _____

L. 1 x 6 = _____

M. 2 x 7 = _____

N. 3 x 6 = _____

O. 5 x 5 = _____

P. 0 x 5 = _____

Q. 3 x 3 = _____

R. 4 x 6 = _____

S. 4 x 4 = _____

T. 7 x 1 = _____

40

Name_____

Divide to discover the answers.

A. $3\overline{)12}$

B. $2\overline{)2}$

C. $5\overline{)35}$

D. $1\overline{)4}$

E. $3\overline{)15}$

F. $6\overline{)36}$

G. $5\overline{)20}$

H. $6\overline{)24}$

I. $5\overline{)10}$

J. $7\overline{)28}$

K. $4\overline{)28}$

L. $4\overline{)12}$

M. $6\overline{)18}$

N. $5\overline{)30}$

O. $2\overline{)8}$

P. $7\overline{)49}$

Q. $1\overline{)6}$

41

Name_____

Multiply to solve the problems.

A. 0 x 5 = ____   B. 1 x 4 = ____   C. 2 x 3 = ____   D. 2 x 5 = ____

E. 2 x 4 = ____   F. 0 x 7 = ____   G. 2 x 2 = ____   H. 5 x 2 = ____

I. 3 x 4 = ____   J. 6 x 1 = ____   K. 2 x 6 = ____   L. 2 x 0 = ____

M. 3 x 2 = ____   N. 3 x 0 = ____   O. 4 x 1 = ____   P. 4 x 2 = ____

Q. 3 x 3 = ____   R. 1 x 3 = ____

S. 0 x 6 = ____   T. 4 x 3 = ____

Name_____

Multiply to solve the problems.

A. 2 x 6 ___   B. 4 x 6 ___

C. 4 x 1 ___   D. 6 x 4 ___

E. 7 x 6 ___   F. 3 x 2 ___

G. 3 x 4 ___   H. 6 x 1 ___

I. 2 x 2 ___   J. 6 x 2 ___

K. 1 x 4 ___   L. 4 x 3 ___

M. 6 x 6 ___   N. 6 x 7 ___

O. 2 x 3 ___   P. 4 x 2 ___

Draw a line from each lock to the key with the correct answer.

A.
2 x 6 =

0

I.
5 x 2 =

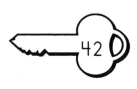
42

B.
3 x 7 =

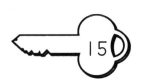
15

J.
4 x 1 =

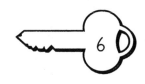
6

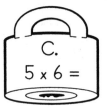
C.
5 x 6 =

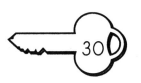
30

K.
3 x 2 =

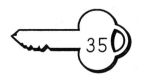
35

D.
4 x 6 =

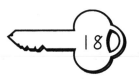
18

L.
7 x 6 =

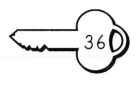
36

E.
7 x 7 =

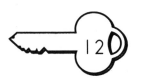
12

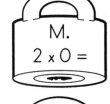
M.
2 x 0 =

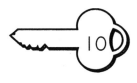
10

F.
0 x 6 =

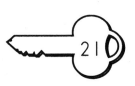
21

N.
6 x 6 =

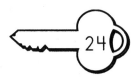
24

G.
6 x 3 =

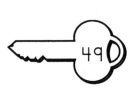
49

O.
6 x 4 =

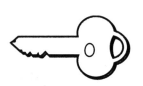
0

H.
5 x 3 =

24

P.
5 x 7 =

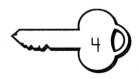
4

Name_____

Divide to solve the problems. Help the kids find their way to school.

A. $30 \div 6 =$ ___   B. $21 \div 7 =$ ___   C. $18 \div 3 =$ ___

G. $12 \div 4 =$ ___   F. $24 \div 6 =$ ___   E. $16 \div 4 =$ ___   D. $42 \div 7 =$ ___

H. $20 \div 4 =$ ___   I. $25 \div 5 =$ ___   J. $28 \div 7 =$ ___   K. $35 \div 5 =$ ___

O. $14 \div 7 =$ ___   N. $36 \div 6 =$ ___   M. $30 \div 5 =$ ___   L. $49 \div 7 =$ ___

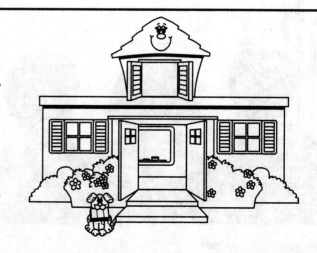

P. $18 \div 6 =$ ___   Q. $28 \div 7 =$ ___

Multiply to solve the problems in the problem list. Use x and = to find the same problems hidden across and down in the puzzle. Circle each hidden problem.

Problem List

7 x 1 = ___   7 x 6 = ___
4 x 4 = ___   6 x 7 = ___   7 x 7 = ___   5 x 5 = ___
0 x 7 = ___   2 x 7 = ___   4 x 2 = ___   6 x 6 = ___
7 x 3 = ___   5 x 3 = ___   2 x 6 = ___   4 x 7 = ___
6 x 3 = ___   7 x 5 = ___   5 x 6 = ___   6 x 4 = ___

6	4	24	20	25	49	56	6	7 x 3 = 21	32	10
8	6	7	42	48	7	12	6	14	36	54	17	9
35	2	21	25	64	5	9	36	25	0	19	8	24
72	0	56	16	9	35	8	16	12	36	7	11	4
8	2	45	2	0	7	0	18	30	5	5	25	x
56	6	49	7	20	15	36	40	17	10	0	3	4 = 16
30	12	3	14	35	11	5	3	15	4	2	8	72
7	13	54	9	63	6	16	8	21	48	5	10	56
1	4	7	28	0	3	17	2	30	21	64	8	7
7	49	24	1	14	18	32	25	7	6	42	56	7
21	45	5	6	30	16	9	54	72	9	30	2	49

Divide to solve the problems in the problem list. Use ÷ and = to find the same problems hidden across and down in the puzzle. Circle each hidden problem and answer.

Problem List

49 ÷ 7 = ____	12 ÷ 4 = ____	16 ÷ 4 = ____	9 ÷ 3 = ____	42 ÷ 6 = ____
18 ÷ 6 = ____	0 ÷ 4 = ____	21 ÷ 7 = ____	35 ÷ 7 = ____	20 ÷ 4 = ____
42 ÷ 7 = ____	28 ÷ 4 = ____	30 ÷ 5 = ____	15 ÷ 3 = ____	
30 ÷ 6 = ____	36 ÷ 6 = ____	25 ÷ 5 = ____	21 ÷ 3 = ____	

```
36   6   7  12   4   3   9   1  (16 ÷ 4 = 4)  15   3
35   4   6   0   3   5  32   3  28   8  36   6  (28
 7  24   4   4  49   3  36  25   5  49   7  12   ÷
 5  42   7   0   5  21   6   5  18  15   3   5   4
15   3   9  10  36   9   6   5  32   4  16   8   = 27  7)
36   9   8  27   3  12   8  24  30   6   5  40   9
18   2   7  18  40   5  36   7  20  30   5   4   6
30  21  12   6   4  20   9  30   5   6  20   3  21
27   3   8   3  49   7   9   3   3  28   4  15   7
 5   7  42   9  16   2  35   7  18   3   5  30   3
36   7   3  27   3   4  42   6   7  49   7   2  16
 4  49   7   7  16   4   1  14  42   7   6   5  32
 2   6   4   5  30  20   7  36   5  40  27   7   2
```

Multiply to solve the problems.

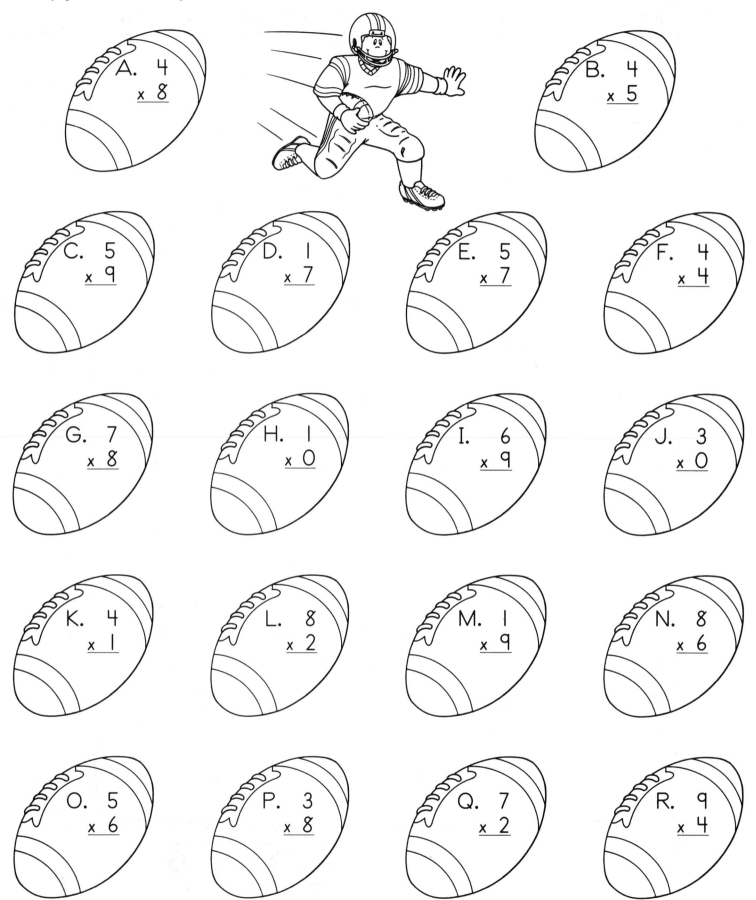

A. 4
x 8

B. 4
x 5

C. 5
x 9

D. 1
x 7

E. 5
x 7

F. 4
x 4

G. 7
x 8

H. 1
x 0

I. 6
x 9

J. 3
x 0

K. 4
x 1

L. 8
x 2

M. 1
x 9

N. 8
x 6

O. 5
x 6

P. 3
x 8

Q. 7
x 2

R. 9
x 4

Name_____

Multiply to solve the problems.

A. 3
  x 7

B. 9
  x 8

C. 1
  x 9

D. 8
  x 7

E. 5
  x 9

F. 8
  x 4

G. 4
  x 1

H. 4
  x 4

I. 3
  x 2

J. 5
  x 7

K. 2
  x 2

L. 8
  x 8

M. 0
  x 6

N. 7
  x 9

O. 2
  x 7

P. 3
  x 3

Q. 4
  x 5

R. 2
  x 7

S. 7
  x 6

T. 3
  x 6

U. 0
  x 8

V. 9
  x 7

W. 8
  x 5

X. 5
  x 6

Y. 4
  x 2

Name_____ **Multiplication and Division Facts: 0 to 9**

Multiply or divide to solve the problems. See if you can get to the "core" of the problems.

A. 8
x 0

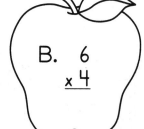
B. 6
x 4

C. 9
x 7

D. 7
x 3

E. 4
x 1

F. 1
x 6

G. 7
x 1

H. 2
x 6

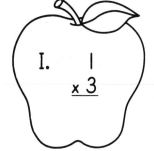
I. 1
x 3

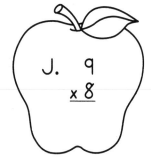
J. 9
x 8

K.
3)27

L.
4)12

M.
2)16

N.
8)56

O.
5)5

P.
4)16

Q.
8)8

R.
9)36

Name_____

Divide to solve the problems. See how many baskets you can make.

A. $2\overline{)18}$ B. $7\overline{)49}$ C. $6\overline{)54}$ D. $8\overline{)32}$

E. $9\overline{)27}$ F. $4\overline{)16}$ G. $8\overline{)72}$ H. $7\overline{)63}$

I. $3\overline{)24}$ J. $4\overline{)28}$ K. $8\overline{)64}$ L. $3\overline{)24}$

M. $9\overline{)45}$ N. $3\overline{)21}$ O. $4\overline{)36}$ P. $6\overline{)42}$ Q. $4\overline{)20}$

R. $8\overline{)56}$ S. $5\overline{)25}$ T. $6\overline{)48}$ U. $2\overline{)12}$ V. $5\overline{)35}$

W. $9\overline{)81}$ X. $8\overline{)40}$ Y. $6\overline{)42}$ Z. $5\overline{)25}$ AA. $7\overline{)14}$

BB. $3\overline{)18}$ CC. $9\overline{)81}$ DD. $2\overline{)16}$ EE. $8\overline{)24}$ FF. $6\overline{)36}$

Name_____ **Multiplication and Division Facts: 0 to 9**

Multiply or divide to solve the problems and "sharpen" your math skills.

A. $9 \times 2 =$ _____

B. $9 \times 0 =$ _____

C. $6 \times 7 =$ _____

D. $1 \times 5 =$ _____

E. $8 \times 4 =$ _____

F. $8 \times 7 =$ _____

G. $8 \times 9 =$ _____

H. $4 \times 4 =$ _____

I. $4 \times 7 =$ _____

J. $6 \times 9 =$ _____

K. $24 \div 8 =$ _____

L. $2 \div 1 =$ _____

M. $28 \div 4 =$ _____

N. $42 \div 6 =$ _____

O. $27 \div 9 =$ _____

P. $64 \div 8 =$ _____

Q. $14 \div 2 =$ _____

R. $21 \div 7 =$ _____

S. $35 \div 5 =$ _____

T. $63 \div 7 =$ _____

U. $49 \div 7 =$ _____

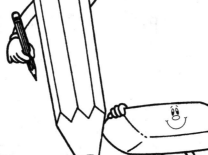

Multiply or divide to help the mountain climber climb the math mountain.

A. $9 \times 8 =$ ___

B. $32 \div 8 =$ ___

C. $40 \div 8 =$ ___   D. $7 \times 5 =$ ___

E. $9 \times 6 =$ ___   F. $45 \div 5 =$ ___

G. $42 \div 7 =$ ___   H. $6 \times 6 =$ ___

I. $5 \times 4 =$ ___   J. $32 \div 4 =$ ___

K. $36 \div 6 =$ ___   L. $12 \div 2 =$ ___

M. $6 \times 3 =$ ___   N. $5 \times 9 =$ ___

O. $8 \times 0 =$ ___   P. $25 \div 5 =$ ___

Q. $28 \div 4 =$ ___   R. $3 \div 3 =$ ___

S. $5 \times 0 =$ ___   T. $4 \times 1 =$ ___   U. $2 \times 6 =$ ___

Divide to solve the problems and then color.

2 = brown   5 = purple   7 = orange   9 = black
6 = green   8 = yellow

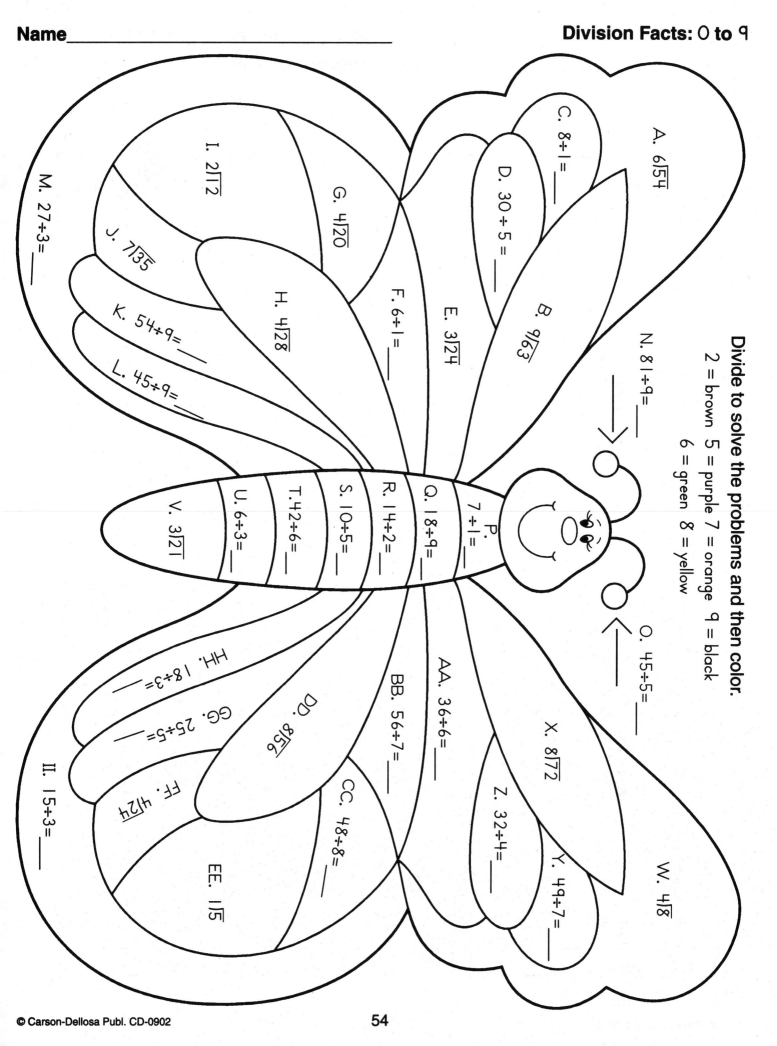

A. 6)54

C. 8÷1= ___

D. 30÷5= ___

B. 9)63

E. 3)24

F. 6÷1= ___

G. 4)20

H. 4)28

I. 2)12

J. 7)35

K. 54÷9= ___

L. 45÷9= ___

M. 27÷3= ___

N. 81÷9= ___

O. 45÷5= ___

P. 7÷1= ___

Q. 18÷9= ___

R. 14÷2= ___

S. 10÷5= ___

T. 42÷6= ___

U. 6÷3= ___

V. 3)21

W. 4)8

X. 8)72

Y. 49÷7= ___

Z. 32÷4= ___

AA. 36÷6= ___

BB. 56÷7= ___

CC. 48÷8= ___

DD. 8)56

EE. 1)5

FF. 4)24

GG. 25÷5= ___

HH. 18÷3= ___

II. 15÷3= ___

Name_____

Divide to solve the problems.

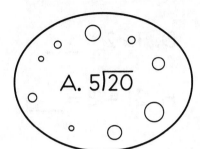
A. 5⟌20

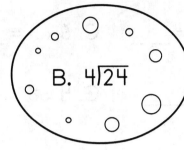
B. 4⟌24

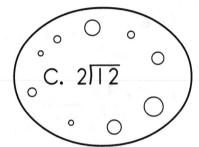
C. 2⟌12

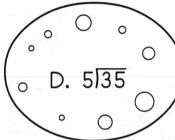
D. 5⟌35

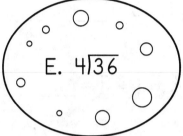
E. 4⟌36

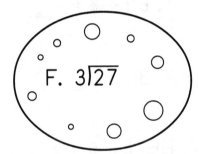
F. 3⟌27

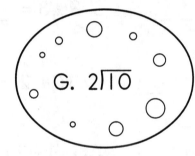
G. 2⟌10

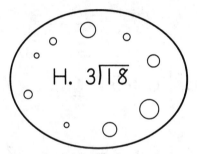
H. 3⟌18

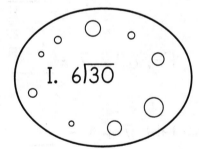
I. 6⟌30

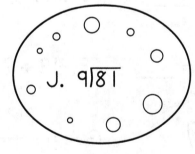
J. 9⟌81

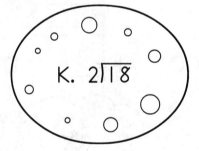
K. 2⟌18

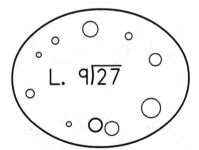
L. 9⟌27

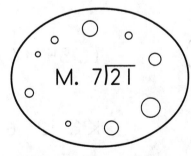
M. 7⟌21

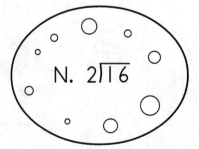
N. 2⟌16

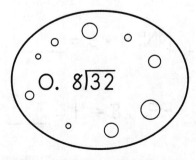
O. 8⟌32

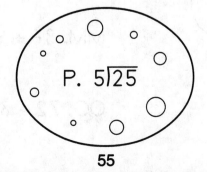
P. 5⟌25

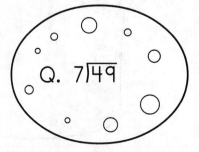
Q. 7⟌49

Name_____

Multiply or divide to solve the problems.

A. $27 \div 3 =$ ___   B. $48 \div 6 =$ ___   C. $6 \times 3 =$ ___   D. $9 \times 2 =$ ___

E. $32 \div 4 =$ ___   F. $9 \div 1 =$ ___   G. $4 \times 8 =$ ___   H. $21 \div 3 =$ ___

I. $3 \times 3 =$ ___   J. $6 \times 6 =$ ___   K. $4 \times 9 =$ ___   L. $8 \times 4 =$ ___

M. $63 \div 9 =$ ___   N. $45 \div 5 =$ ___   O. $8 \div 1 =$ ___   P. $2 \times 9 =$ ___

Q. $56 \div 7 =$ ___   R. $3 \times 6 =$ ___   S. $8 \times 3 =$ ___   T. $64 \div 8 =$ ___

U. $40 \div 5 =$ ___   V. $72 \div 9 =$ ___   W. $16 \div 2 =$ ___   X. $3 \times 8 =$ ___

Y. $56 \div 8 =$ ___   Z. $6 \times 4 =$ ___   AA. $4 \times 2 =$ ___   BB. $81 \div 9 =$ ___

CC. $7 \times 1 =$ ___   DD. $8 \times 2 =$ ___   EE. $49 \div 7 =$ ___   FF. $63 \div 7 =$ ___

GG. $4 \times 4 =$ ___   HH. $7 \div 1 =$ ___

II. $54 \div 6 =$ ___   JJ. $9 \times 1 =$ ___

KK. $42 \times 6 =$ ___   LL. $14 \div 2 =$ ___

MM. $36 \div 4 =$ ___   NN. $4 \times 6 =$ ___

OO. $72 \div 8 =$ ___   PP. $28 \div 4 =$ ___

Name_____

Multiply to solve the problems.

A. $6 \times 3 =$ ___

B. $5 \times 9 =$ ___   C. $7 \times 7 =$ ___

D. $9 \times 9 =$ ___   E. $5 \times 6 =$ ___   F. $6 \times 7 =$ ___

G. $4 \times 9 =$ ___   H. $4 \times 8 =$ ___   I. $4 \times 6 =$ ___

J. $6 \times 9 =$ ___   K. $8 \times 8 =$ ___   L. $7 \times 4 =$ ___

M. $8 \times 6 =$ ___   N. $5 \times 8 =$ ___   O. $3 \times 9 =$ ___

P. $4 \times 4 =$ ___   Q. $3 \times 8 =$ ___   R. $8 \times 4 =$ ___

Name_____

Divide to solve the problems.

A. $81 \div 9 = $ _____

B. $64 \div 8 = $ _____

C. $54 \div 9 = $ _____

D. $49 \div 7 = $ _____

E. $42 \div 7 = $ _____

F. $45 \div 5 = $ _____

G. $36 \div 9 = $ _____

H. $32 \div 8 = $ _____

I. $27 \div 3 = $ _____

J. $12 \div 3 = $ _____

K. $25 \div 5 = $ _____

L. $18 \div 2 = $ _____

M. $12 \div 4 = $ _____

N. $63 \div 9 = $ _____

O. $35 \div 5 = $ _____

P. $40 \div 8 = $ _____

Q. $18 \div 9 = $ _____

R. $24 \div 4 = $ _____

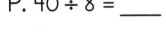

S. $14 \div 7 = $ _____

T. $56 \div 8 = $ _____

U. $48 \div 6 = $ _____

V. $16 \div 2 = $ _____

W. $21 \div 3 = $ _____

X. $15 \div 3 = $ _____

Y. $28 \div 4 = $ _____

Z. $30 \div 6 = $ _____

Multiply to sovle the problems in the problem list. Use x and = to find the same problems hidden across and down in the puzzle. Circle each hidden problem.

		Problem List		
9 x 1 = ____	7 x 7 = ____		5 x 8 = ____	3 x 6 = ____
8 x 5 = ____	6 x 6 = ____	9 x 2 = ____	9 x 9 = ____	0 x 8 = ____
7 x 5 = ____	7 x 4 = ____	8 x 8 = ____	3 x 8 = ____	9 x 4 = ____
9 x 3 = ____	8 x 4 = ____	9 x 7 = ____	4 x 9 = ____	9 x 5 = ____

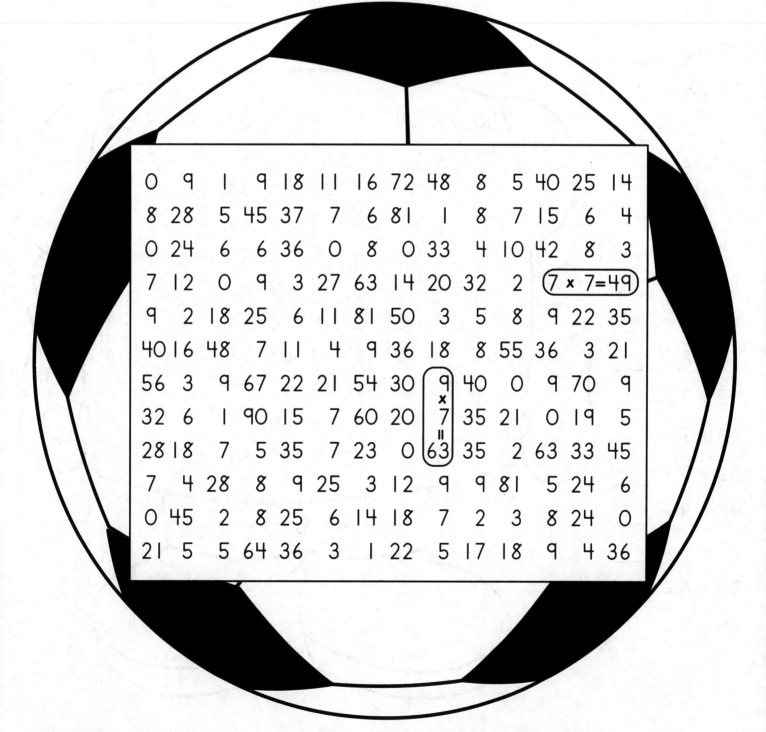

Name_____

Divide to solve the problems in the problem list. Use ÷ and = to find the same problems hidden across and down in the puzzle. Circle each hidden problem.

Problem List

$81 \div 9 =$ ___

$9 \div 1 =$ ___

$27 \div 3 =$ ___

$36 \div 4 =$ ___

$18 \div 2 =$ ___

$24 \div 6 =$ ___

$32 \div 8 =$ ___

$18 \div 3 =$ ___

$16 \div 4 =$ ___

$40 \div 5 =$ ___

$48 \div 8 =$ ___

$42 \div 7 =$ ___

$63 \div 7 =$ ___

$56 \div 8 =$ ___

$45 \div 9 =$ ___

$72 \div 9 =$ ___

$54 \div 6 =$ ___

$64 \div 8 =$ ___

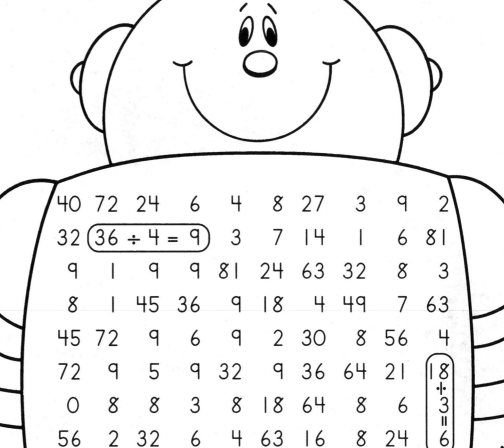

40	72	24	6	4	8	27	3	9	2
32	36 ÷ 4 = 9		3	7	14	1	6	81
9	1	9	9	81	24	63	32	8	3
8	1	45	36	9	18	4	49	7	63
45	72	9	6	9	2	30	8	56	4
72	9	5	9	32	9	36	64	21	18÷3=6
0	8	8	3	8	18	64	8	6	
56	2	32	6	4	63	16	8	24	
8	45	63	7	9	42	7	6	4	42
7	2	54	6	9	6	15	16	4	4
3	40	5	8	4	8	64	48	8	6

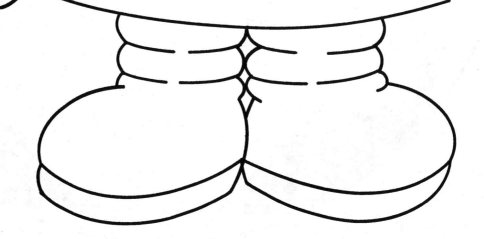

Answer Key

Page 1   Multiplication Facts: 0 to 5
A. 12, 3, 4, 25, 15, 0, 8, 4, 0, 10
B. 25, 8, 0, 16, 5, 6, 20, 10, 0, 9
C. 0, 3, 5, 20, 0, 1, 4, 0, 0, 2
D. 6, 12, 0, 15, 10, 16, 0, 3, 10, 2
E. 0, 3, 2, 6, 0, 4, 12, 0, 15, 5
F. 8, 0, 0, 8, 9, 5, 1, 4, 0, 0
G. 20, 2, 0, 5, 0, 16, 2, 10, 5, 8
H. 0, 10, 4, 0, 6, 3, 15, 0, 4, 12
I. 20, 0, 6, 12, 1, 6, 15, 2, 4, 25
J. 12, 0, 20, 4, 15, 0, 20, 3, 8, 9

Page 2   Multiplication Facts: 0 to 5
A. 3, 10, 4, 12, 20, 0, 9, 0, 6, 12
B. 0, 25, 4, 8, 1, 10, 16, 2, 0, 15
C. 5, 0, 12, 6, 5, 0, 6, 10, 3, 2
D. 0, 9, 5, 0, 3, 20, 8, 0, 1, 25
E. 16, 4, 0, 4, 12, 0, 15, 2, 0, 15
F. 5, 9, 0, 10, 4, 4, 20, 0, 0, 15
G. 8, 2, 4, 1, 10, 6, 3, 12, 6, 0
H. 2, 0, 5, 3, 15, 0, 20, 0, 25, 0
I. 0, 8, 15, 4, 8, 0, 12, 20, 0, 4
J. 8, 0, 0, 6, 5, 3, 20, 10, 2, 16

Page 3   Multiplication Facts: 0 to 7
A. 12, 0, 35, 30, 9, 21, 5, 16, 24, 20
B. 0, 49, 6, 1, 18, 10, 30, 4, 0, 35
C. 30, 18, 12, 7, 0, 28, 15, 4, 42, 15
D. 35, 4, 0, 6, 12, 0, 6, 20, 14, 12
E. 2, 15, 28, 0, 8, 36, 20, 6, 10, 0
F. 14, 15, 8, 25, 6, 12, 10, 0, 21, 24
G. 20, 8, 0, 42, 18, 12, 14, 49, 3, 4
H. 2, 21, 36, 16, 10, 0, 35, 24, 3, 42
I. 0, 12, 7, 28, 18, 5, 0, 24, 8, 9
J. 0, 6, 42, 12, 0, 28, 25, 21, 30, 14

Page 4   Multiplication Facts: 0 to 7
A. 36, 3, 0, 8, 0, 16, 30, 6, 18, 20
B. 30, 5, 7, 21, 28, 6, 24, 0, 6, 12
C. 20, 9, 49, 8, 30, 0, 14, 18, 28, 42
D. 25, 0, 3, 42, 15, 24, 35, 2, 0, 35
E. 21, 0, 12, 20, 3, 0, 28, 10, 7, 12
F. 5, 15, 0, 21, 12, 35, 4, 12, 0, 8
G. 49, 10, 24, 0, 20, 2, 12, 42, 4, 6
H. 16, 12, 6, 0, 1, 42, 10, 0, 18, 21
I. 2, 9, 6, 4, 36, 7, 0, 28, 14, 30
J. 35, 0, 5, 15, 14, 4, 18, 24, 25, 15

Page 5   Multiplication Facts: 0 to 9
A. 0, 10, 0, 18, 20, 14, 42, 18, 42, 1
B. 40, 6, 24, 8, 63, 0, 3, 21, 6, 32
C. 35, 9, 4, 6, 0, 15, 81, 12, 45, 0
D. 16, 36, 28, 0, 63, 9, 25, 2, 0, 8
E. 0, 64, 15, 24, 4, 5, 7, 32, 0, 27
F. 7, 12, 40, 3, 0, 6, 35, 0, 18, 8
G. 18, 0, 0, 20, 16, 56, 0, 54, 0, 36
H. 72, 2, 45, 28, 0, 4, 21, 72, 9, 56
I. 24, 54, 8, 30, 12, 0, 10, 16, 0, 49
J. 5, 27, 12, 0, 48, 30, 36, 24, 14, 48

Page 6   Multiplication Facts: 0 to 9
A. 16, 32, 3, 42, 0, 27, 8, 30, 0, 35
B. 14, 18, 0, 54, 0, 21, 45, 24, 40, 5
C. 4, 64, 0, 24, 10, 36, 0, 56, 16, 9
D. 15, 48, 6, 32, 12, 8, 28, 0, 18, 9
E. 12, 6, 0, 35, 0, 72, 36, 7, 0, 20
F. 0, 72, 3, 49, 10, 6, 0, 2, 56, 25
G. 30, 27, 0, 63, 8, 5, 1, 8, 4, 63
H. 40, 4, 21, 15, 45, 14, 36, 12, 24, 0
I. 2, 48, 0, 9, 81, 16, 0, 42, 6, 20
J. 28, 0, 54, 24, 0, 12, 0, 18, 7, 18

Page 7   Multiplication Facts: 0 to 9
A. 63, 32, 27, 30, 0, 12, 6, 16, 6, 0
B. 12, 25, 0, 56, 9, 0, 81, 0, 54, 42
C. 63, 12, 21, 0, 35, 0, 3, 45, 20, 14
D. 7, 27, 6, 0, 40, 0, 4, 36, 0, 48
E. 28, 24, 18, 6, 10, 2, 48, 9, 0, 18
F. 15, 20, 0, 56, 8, 16, 7, 12, 0, 8
G. 40, 13, 24, 0, 35, 72, 5, 16, 36, 10
H. 0, 54, 0, 21, 2, 64, 24, 8, 0, 36
I. 49, 45, 0, 14, 1, 4, 42, 15, 72, 9
J. 8, 30, 4, 24, 32, 18, 5, 0, 28, 18

Page 8   Multiplication Facts: 0 to 9
A. 24, 54, 24, 0, 2, 9, 0, 27, 20, 8
B. 6, 42, 0, 5, 8, 24, 21, 0, 24, 45
C. 48, 16, 0, 3, 12, 35, 2, 48, 15, 72
D. 63, 1, 0, 14, 20, 6, 0, 45, 0, 16
E. 12, 7, 72, 42, 0, 14, 35, 21, 6, 4
F. 12, 10, 8, 40, 18, 30, 36, 0, 81, 5
G. 64, 0, 9, 27, 6, 32, 0, 15, 56, 36
H. 0, 18, 4, 7, 0, 63, 16, 9, 3, 56
I. 12, 28, 25, 0, 32, 40, 0, 8, 0, 18
J. 30, 4, 10, 36, 49, 18, 0, 54, 0, 28

Page 9   Multiplication Facts: 12 to 9
A. 18, 14, 3, 42, 0, 20, 9, 12, 63, 20
B. 8, 5, 0, 4, 0, 32, 6, 56, 0, 45
C. 5, 27, 8, 0, 30, 0, 56, 16, 15, 0
D. 42, 10, 18, 16, 32, 2, 40, 0, 28, 24
E. 36, 0, 21, 48, 6, 7, 15, 54, 8, 24
F. 6, 64, 28, 3, 10, 0, 12, 4, 0, 14
G. 25, 0, 24, 2, 54, 0, 12, 35, 9, 72
H. 72, 4, 0, 7, 24, 0, 27, 45, 8, 49
I. 0, 48, 0, 21, 1, 40, 0, 63, 6, 16
J. 18, 30, 18, 36, 0, 81, 36, 12, 35, 9

Page 10   Multiplication Facts: 0 to 9
A. 28, 24, 3, 45, 4, 32, 6, 48, 0, 25
B. 8, 0, 0, 12, 15, 18, 21, 0, 72, 14
C. 20, 0, 56, 0, 5, 28, 6, 9, 24, 0
D. 7, 36, 8, 42, 0, 0, 45, 42, 3, 12
E. 0, 40, 6, 30, 1, 36, 0, 4, 12, 20
F. 49, 27, 5, 0, 36, 4, 12, 24, 0, 10
G. 27, 9, 0, 16, 0, 40, 81, 2, 64, 0
H. 16, 6, 54, 7, 35, 32, 0, 72, 21, 63
I. 35, 0, 24, 9, 15, 18, 48, 14, 2, 63
J. 16, 18, 0, 56, 10, 18, 8, 54, 8, 30

Answer Key

Page 11   Multiplication Facts: 0 to 9

A. 9, 40, 10, 35, 28
B. 0, 0, 48, 0, 18
C. 54, 28, 0, 16, 0
D. 24, 7, 21, 3, 15
E. 81, 27, 0, 63. 0
F. 3, 32, 35, 10, 2
G. 36, 0, 7, 0, 18
H. 12, 56, 8, 40, 2
I. 24, 72, 5, 0, 21
J. 8, 30, 0, 12, 0
K. 63, 0, 36, 6, 18
L. 0, 54, 6, 72, 0
M. 14, 12, 0, 15, 24
N. 6, 45, 8, 1, 49
O. 30, 0, 25, 18, 16
P. 27, 6, 5, 16, 4
Q. 4, 9, 36, 0, 42
R. 32, 20, 42, 45, 20
S. 64, 48, 0, 9, 56
T. 12, 4, 14, 24, 8

Page 12   Multiplication Facts: 0 to 9

A. 42, 24, 10, 0, 35
B. 5, 72, 16, 7, 8
C. 42, 0, 6, 36, 18
D. 30, 18, 0, 24, 0
E. 54, 8, 81, 0, 9
F. 2, 35, 18, 3, 20
G. 0, 21, 0, 63, 9
H. 12, 32, 36, 6, 25
I. 16, 0, 40, 4, 28
J. 0, 1, 6, 54, 12
K. 48, 8, 5, 0, 4
L. 15, 4, 0, 16, 64
M. 0, 32, 30, 14, 18
N. 45, 3, 0, 56, 8
O. 27, 14, 0, 2, 0
P. 72, 0, 9, 45, 21
Q. 24, 63, 7, 27, 20
R. 49, 0, 40, 0, 48
S. 36, 12, 56, 0, 15
T. 6, 10, 12, 28, 24

Page 13   Division Facts: 0 to 5

A. 1, 2, 5, 0, 3, 3, 2, 2, 4, 5
B. 5, 4, 2, 1, 5, 2, 1, 5, 5, 4
C. 2, 3, 1, 1, 0, 1, 5, 4, 4, 0
D. 5, 5, 4, 0, 1, 1, 4, 5, 3, 0
E. 4, 0, 2, 3, 2, 4, 3, 5, 4, 3
F. 0, 3, 3, 4, 5, 2, 5, 1, 5, 4
G. 1, 4, 5, 1, 0, 2, 3, 3, 0, 3
H. 4, 0, 5, 1, 5, 4, 2, 3, 2, 4
I. 4, 1, 3, 2, 1, 2, 0, 1, 3, 5
J. 1, 1, 3, 3, 2, 4, 2, 0, 2, 0

Page 14   Division Facts: 0 to 5

A. 1, 4, 3, 0, 2, 2, 1, 3, 3, 3
B. 2, 2, 1, 3, 1, 3, 5, 3, 3, 4
C. 2, 5, 3, 1, 4, 5, 3, 5, 3, 0
D. 4, 4, 3, 3, 1, 3, 0, 5, 1, 4
E. 5, 4, 0, 1, 2, 5, 1, 1, 3, 5
F. 2, 5, 2, 4, 2, 0, 3, 3, 0, 4
G. 2, 0, 4, 5, 0, 4, 2, 1, 4, 1
H. 2, 2, 2, 4, 1, 4, 5, 5, 4, 1
I. 5, 1, 4, 2, 2, 1, 0, 5, 5, 5
J. 1, 0, 5, 1, 3, 2, 4, 5, 2, 4

Page 15   Division Facts: 0 to 7

A. 4, 1, 7, 6, 2, 2, 4, 3, 2, 1
B. 7, 4, 1, 5, 0, 4, 6, 4, 7, 6
C. 3 4, 3, 6, 7, 7, 1, 0, 2, 1
D. 2, 0, 3, 2, 5, 4, 1, 5, 2, 4
E. 6, 3, 4, 1, 3, 3, 5, 6, 4, 0
F. 7, 3, 2, 6, 3, 7, 0, 7, 6, 1
G. 0, 6, 2, 5, 7, 3, 5, 1, 5, 6
H. 6, 5, 5, 5, 1, 7, 1, 2, 1, 5
I. 7, 3, 5, 1, 0, 7, 2, 4, 7, 6
J. 5, 5, 6, 2, 2, 4, 4, 3, 3, 6

Page 16   Division Facts: 0 to 7

A. 2, 7, 6, 3, 5, 4, 7, 4, 3, 2
B. 3, 4, 1, 6, 6, 1, 2, 5, 5, 4
C. 6, 1, 3, 0, 7, 6, 2, 1, 2, 5
D. 4, 6, 2, 4, 6, 1, 3, 4, 4, 7
E. 5, 6, 0, 6, 3, 3, 2, 1, 6, 7
F. 1, 2, 3, 5, 5, 5, 1, 0, 3, 7
G. 7, 6, 2, 0, 5, 7, 3, 3, 5, 7
H. 4, 1, 4, 1, 2, 0, 3, 2, 1, 5
I. 7, 1, 2, 5, 5, 4, 0, 5, 7, 7
J. 7, 4, 2, 3, 1, 4, 6, 6, 0, 6

Page 17   Division Facts: 0 to 9

A. 9, 3, 2, 4, 7, 2, 2, 3, 6, 5
B. 3, 5, 0, 8, 6, 6, 6, 6, 4, 8, 2
C. 8, 7, 2, 1, 0, 9, 7, 1, 9, 3
D. 3, 4, 0, 8, 4, 5, 6, 1, 0, 9
E. 5, 5, 0, 9, 5, 6, 1, 4, 3, 7
F. 9, 0, 2, 2, 9, 6, 1, 6, 9, 4
G. 4, 8, 1, 5, 4, 0, 3, 2, 7, 7
H. 3, 2, 6, 1, 1, 4, 8, 3, 6, 9
I. 7, 5, 5, 8, 0, 8, 3, 9, 2, 4
J. 1, 8, 7, 5, 5, 0, 8, 7, 3, 4

Page 18   Division Facts: 0 to 9

A. 7, 4, 1, 2, 7, 4, 3, 4, 8, 8
B. 8, 9, 2, 0, 6, 8, 6, 6, 3, 5
C. 6, 4, 8, 1, 2, 8, 0, 1, 5, 4
D. 3, 8, 1, 3, 7, 4, 2, 6, 1, 0
E. 9, 5, 3, 3, 8, 0, 4, 2, 4, 6
F. 7, 4, 0, 1, 7, 3, 8, 5, 2, 7
G. 9, 0, 4, 1, 9, 5, 1, 7, 8, 2
H. 5, 4, 4, 0, 5, 3, 6, 1, 3, 5
I. 2, 7, 3, 9, 2, 7, 9, 6, 0, 9
J. 6, 5, 8, 8, 9, 8, 7, 0, 9, 2

Page 19   Division Facts: 0 to 9

A. 3, 6, 4, 6, 8, 6, 1, 7, 6, 4
B. 2, 6, 2, 7, 3, 5, 0, 9, 1, 2
C. 0, 2, 8, 8, 3, 9, 1, 6, 4, 9
D. 4, 4, 9, 1, 0, 7, 1, 3, 3, 0
E. 7, 2, 6, 5, 5, 6, 5, 5, 2, 1
F. 8, 4, 1, 5, 6, 8, 0, 5, 4, 6
G. 2, 8, 0, 3, 1, 0, 3, 9, 7, 3
H. 2, 2, 8, 9, 1, 8, 4, 7, 9, 5
I. 3, 5, 4, 2, 4, 9, 7, 0, 2, 5
J. 9, 7, 7, 3, 0, 7, 9, 8, 8, 6

Page 20   Division Facts: 0 to 9

A. 2, 7, 2, 7, 5, 4, 0, 5, 9, 3
B. 6, 2, 3, 3, 8, 0, 8, 9, 7, 5
C. 7, 7, 8, 1, 4, 3, 1, 8, 5, 5
D. 3, 0, 5, 3, 1, 8, 0, 6, 4, 3
E. 7, 2, 1, 6, 1, 5, 4, 1, 8, 9
F. 3, 4, 3, 0, 1, 9, 0, 4, 7, 7
G. 7, 5, 8, 6, 9, 0, 1, 8, 4, 0
H. 8, 9, 9, 7, 3, 3, 7, 4, 2, 2
I. 2, 6, 4, 1, 2, 0, 6, 7, 9, 4
J. 6, 9, 6, 6, 9, 2, 5, 6, 2, 5

Answer Key

Page 21   Division Facts: 0 to 9
A. 4, 2, 2, 8, 1, 5, 5, 8, 7, 5
B. 9, 3, 3, 0, 9, 6, 1, 5, 7, 6
C. 0, 4, 2, 9, 3, 8, 8, 6, 2, 3
D. 3, 2, 5, 6, 0, 7, 1, 5, 6, 1
E. 3, 4, 6, 7, 8, 9, 0, 4, 1, 3
F. 7, 8, 7, 8, 6, 1, 8, 2, 5, 5
G. 0, 3, 2, 1, 0, 9, 9, 5, 0, 4
H. 3, 9, 4, 2, 8, 7, 8, 2, 7, 4
I. 3, 4, 0, 8, 6, 3, 5, 5, 1, 6
J. 7, 9, 3, 4, 9, 1, 0, 4, 8, 7

Page 22   Division Facts: 0 to 9
A. 5, 9, 6, 6, 1, 3, 2, 5, 6, 9
B. 7, 8, 4, 5, 2, 5, 8, 1, 3, 3
C. 7, 1, 2, 9, 3, 0, 5, 3, 0, 7
D. 0, 8, 8, 0, 1, 9, 8, 2, 7, 4
E. 2, 6, 9, 9, 4, 9, 1, 8, 4, 0
F. 6, 0, 5, 2, 6, 0, 1, 7, 6, 4
G. 3, 4, 6, 0, 2, 9, 2, 2, 1, 8
H. 6, 5, 7, 8, 8, 0, 8, 3, 7, 4
I. 6, 3, 7, 8, 4, 5 1, 4, 7, 6
J. 7, 3, 4, 8, 9, 3, 5, 1, 5, 4

Page 23   Division Facts: 0 to 9
A. 6, 8, 5, 2, 7   K. 1, 9, 1, 2, 0
B. 3, 3, 4, 7, 4   L. 4, 9, 0, 7, 4
C. 5, 6, 3, 7, 4   M. 5, 4, 9, 0, 2
D. 7, 3, 3, 5, 3   N. 5, 8, 0, 7, 6
E. 5, 8, 9, 0, 5   O. 5, 6, 2, 0, 2
F. 1, 3, 2, 7, 8   P. 1, 0, 4, 8, 8
G. 5, 7, 8, 1, 5   Q. 9, 3, 6, 5, 7
H. 3, 3, 9, 9, 2   R. 8, 4, 1, 0, 2
I. 6, 1, 3, 2, 0   S. 9, 9, 6, 8, 3
J. 1, 7, 4, 6, 4   T. 9, 6, 1, 8, 2

Page 24   Division Facts: 0 to 9
A. 4, 8, 2, 6, 7   K. 5, 4, 8, 7, 0
B. 8, 3, 3, 8, 8   L. 1, 7, 0, 1, 7
C. 3, 9, 6, 1, 7   M. 5, 5, 1, 4, 3
D. 5, 4, 4, 6, 9   N. 0, 6, 6, 3, 6
E. 8, 6, 9, 1, 3   O. 4, 1, 9, 0, 9
F. 7, 6, 2, 2, 4   P. 5, 3, 2, 1, 7
G. 9, 2, 8, 3, 3   Q. 1, 7, 9, 0, 7
H. 8, 4, 2, 0, 8   R. 8, 5, 0, 9, 6
I. 3, 8, 0, 7, 5   S. 5, 9, 7, 6, 4
J. 0, 1, 2, 2, 7   T. 5, 2, 4, 3, 5

Page 25   Multiplication and
**   Division Facts: 0 to 9**
A. 0, 4, 12, 5, 21, 7, 35, 1, 7, 4
B. 7, 16, 6, 3, 0, 64, 2, 8, 9, 4
C. 8, 18, 45, 0, 6, 2, 0, 6, 15, 63
D. 7, 4, 0, 0, 15, 4, 0, 30, 27, 1
E. 1, 18, 63, 3, 5, 0, 49, 0, 2, 40
F. 0, 1, 3, 0, 1, 7, 2, 20, 3, 9
G. 9, 36, 0, 8, 2, 16, 9, 6, 16, 0
H. 8, 10, 4, 9, 0, 6, 0, 4, 5, 54
I. 35, 6, 2, 54, 8, 8, 3, 0, 0, 7
J. 9, 8, 0, 1, 72, 56, 9, 0, 20, 8

Page 26   Multiplication and
**   Division Facts: 0 to 9**
A. 8, 0, 5, 7, 5, 0, 9, 2, 15, 56
B. 0, 21, 36, 0, 0, 36, 0, 24, 1, 3
C. 9, 0, 3, 2, 18, 4, 6, 10, 6, 28
D. 40, 7, 0, 5, 28, 4, 3, 27, 6, 2
E. 9, 2, 9, 63, 0, 1, 3, 0, 8, 24
F. 45, 7, 16, 0, 8, 24, 6, 18, 4, 42
G. 4, 3, 3, 40, 1, 0, 6, 5, 16, 4
H. 0, 7, 8, 2, 1, 0, 4, 25, 54, 7
I. 0, 0, 6, 8, 0, 3, 81, 0, 8, 9
J. 9, 0, 14, 30, 8, 48, 4, 7, 14, 9

Page 29
A. 1	B. 0	C. 2	D. 10	E. 15
F. 4	G. 5	H. 6	I. 0	J. 5
K. 8	L. 3	M. 15	N. 0	O. 2
P. 4	Q. 25	R. 12	S. 0	T. 9

Page 30
A. 12	B. 3	C. 4	D. 25	E. 0
F. 0	G. 8	H. 5	I. 20	J. 0
K. 10	L. 0	M. 6	N. 12	O. 4
P. 16	Q. 0	R. 10	S. 2	T. 15
U. 9	V. 0	W. 0	X. 15	

Page 31
A. 5	B. 2	C. 5		
D. 5	E. 0	F. 5		
G. 0	H. 5	I. 5		
J. 2	K. 0			
L. 1	M. 4	N. 0		
O. 4	P. 5	Q. 4	R. 2	S. 4
T. 0	U. 1			

Page 32
A. 2	B. 5		
C. 1	D. 3		
E. 4	F. 2		
G. 0	H. 1	I. 5	J. 5
K. 2	L. 5	M. 4	N. 1
O. 3	P. 1	Q. 4	R. 5
S. 2	T. 3	U. 4	V. 2

Page 33
A. 0	B. 2	
C. 1	D. 4	
E. 3	F. 5	
G. 4	H. 4	I. 4
J. 5	K. 5	L. 3
M. 4	N. 5	O. 5
P. 4	Q. 5	R. 3
S. 4	T. 5	U. 0

Page 34
A. 0	G. 12
B. 8	H. 4
C. 9	I. 6
D. 5	J. 0
E. 25	K. 10
F. 16	L. 20

Page 35

Answer Key

Page 36

Page 37
A. 12　B. 3　C. 25　D. 8
E. 4　F. 6　G. 0　H. 14
I. 10　J. 0　K. 20　L. 2
M. 15　N. 6　O. 0　P. 12
Q. 9　R. 21　S. 24　T. 10
U. 20　V. 18
W. 30　X. 24
Y. 18　Z. 36

Page 38
A. 0　B. 6　C. 4　D. 6
E. 0　F. 0　G. 6　H. 15
I. 14　J. 12　K. 16　L. 35
M. 24　N. 9　O. 8　P. 20
Q. 18　R. 24　S. 14　T. 30
U. 7　V. 12　W. 12　X. 20

Page 39
A. 4　B. 1　C. 6
D. 2　E. 3　F. 4　G. 7　H. 7
I. 6　J. 4　K. 3　L. 7　M. 2
N. 7　O. 6　P. 1　Q. 7　R. 5
S. 7　T. 6

Page 40
A. 12　B. 35　C. 21
D. 0　E. 42　F. 15
G. 0　H. 0　I. 12
J. 10　K. 20　L. 6
M. 14　N. 18
O. 25　P. 0
Q. 9　R. 24
S. 16　T. 7

Page 41
A. 4　B. 1
C. 7　D. 4　E. 5
F. 6　G. 4　H. 4　I. 2
J. 4　K. 7　L. 3　M. 3
N. 6　O. 4　P. 7　Q. 6

Page 42
A. 0　B. 4　C. 6　D. 10
E. 8　F. 0　G. 4　H. 10
I. 12　J. 6　K. 12　L. 0
M. 6　N. 0　O. 4　P. 8
Q. 9　R. 3
S. 0　T. 12

Page 43
A. 12　B. 24
C. 4　D. 24
E. 42　F. 6
G. 12　H. 6
I. 4　J. 12
K. 4　L. 12
M. 36　N. 42
O. 6　P. 8

Page 44
A. 12　I. 10
B. 21　J. 4
C. 30　K. 6
D. 24　L. 42
E. 49　M. 0
F. 0　N. 36
G. 18　O. 24
H. 15　P. 35

Page 45
A. 5　B. 3　C. 6
D. 6　E. 4　F. 4　G. 3
H. 5　I. 5　J. 4　K. 7
L. 7　M. 6　N. 6　O. 2
P. 3　Q. 4

Page 46

Page 47

Page 48
A. 32　B. 20
C. 45　D. 7　E. 35　F. 16
G. 56　H. 0　I. 54　J. 0
K. 4　L. 16　M. 9　N. 48
O. 30　P. 24　Q. 14　R. 36

Page 49
A. 21　B. 72　C. 9　D. 56　E. 45
F. 32　G. 4　H. 16　I. 6　J. 35
K. 4　L. 64　M. 0　N. 63　O. 14
P. 9　Q. 20　R. 14　S. 42　T. 18
U. 0　V. 63　W. 40　X. 30　Y. 8

Page 50
A. 0　B. 24　C. 63　D. 21
E. 4　F. 6　G. 7　H. 12
I. 3　J. 72　K. 9　L. 3
M. 8　N. 7　O. 1　P. 4
Q. 1　R. 4

Page 51
A. 9　B. 7　C. 9　D. 4
E. 3　F. 4　G. 9　H. 9
I. 8　J. 7　K. 8　L. 8
M. 5　N. 7　O. 9　P. 7　Q. 5
R. 7　S. 5　T. 8　U. 6　V. 7
W. 9　X. 5　Y. 7　Z. 5　AA. 2
BB. 6　CC. 9　DD. 8　EE. 3　FF. 6

64